Destroying Everything Bad in the Land:
Implementing Charles Spurgeon's
Gospel-Centered Ethic Toward
The Vulnerable in Society

Destroying Everything Bad in the Land: Implementing Charles Spurgeon's Gospel-Centered Ethic Toward The Vulnerable in Society

Matthew R. Perry

AN IMPRINT OF THE
GLOBAL CENTER FOR RELIGIOUS RESEARCH
1312 17TH STREET • SUITE 549
DENVER, COLORADO 80202

INFO@GCRR.ORG • GCRR.ORG

GCRR Press
An imprint of the Global Center for Religious Research
1312 17th Street Suite 549
Denver, CO 80202
www.gcrr.org

Copyright © 2023 by Matthew R. Perry

DOI: 10.33929/GCRRPress.2023.01

Typesetter / Copyeditor / Proofreader: Jaclyn Prout
Cover Design: Abdullah Al Mahmud
                  fiverr.com/mahmuddidar

Library of Congress Cataloging-in-Publication Data

Destroying everything bad in the land : Implementing Charles Spurgeon's gospel-centered ethic toward the vulnerable in society / Matthew R. Perry
p. cm.
Includes bibliographic references and index.
ISBN (Print): 978-1-959281-06-1
ISBN (eBook): 978-1-959281-07-8
1. Spurgeon, C. H. (Charles Haddon), 1834–1892.   2. Church and social problems—United States.   3. Church renewal.   4. Christianity—Essence, genius, nature.   5. Christianity—21st century.   I. Title.

BR121.3.P47   2023

CB

To my beautiful, gracious, godly wife Cindy,
You make me glad.

And my four children,
You bring me joy.

And to the risen Lord Jesus Christ,
Your mercy and grace still stun me.

When the days are weary, the long nights dreary
I know my Savior cares.
–Frank E. Graeff

Advanced Endorsements

Christians today are asking all kinds of questions relating to nationalism, racism, and religious liberty. But we're not the first ones to deal with such questions. 180 years ago, Charles Haddon Spurgeon dealt with these very issues. From British imperialism, to slavery, to living under a state church, Spurgeon sought to help Christians think biblically and live faithfully. For those seeking to learn from the past, Matthew Perry's study invites us to walk alongside a faithful pastor from church history and glean his wisdom for our day.

—Geoff Chang, Assistant Professor of Historical Theology,
Curator of the Spurgeon Library,
Midwestern Baptist Theological Seminary

Matthew Perry in his important work *Destroying Everything Bad in the Land* interacts with the best of Spurgeon scholarship in offering a unique book demonstrating academic rigor with practical considerations. Perry offers principles for Christians to apply, drawn from Spurgeon's life and ministry, that are instructive in learning how to better love one's neighbor. Spurgeon's ethical outlook and practices are a reflection of his biblically-driven theology that was centered on the gospel of Christ. He had no interest in the church merely engaging in societal programs of benevolence. Spurgeon's ultimate objective was to promote the gospel through his ministries to the vulnerable. I think you will find Perry's book a helpful contribution to Spurgeon studies and useful to inform your own ministry to the "least of these."

— Ray Rhodes, Jr., author of *Susie: The Life and Legacy of Susannah Spurgeon* and *Yours, till Heaven: The Untold Love Story of Charles and Susannah Spurgeon*

Contents

Preface

Why another book on the life and ministry of Charles Haddon Spurgeon (1834–1892)? Simply put, evangelicals need help navigating through some serious issues that have arisen in recent times. The rise of Donald Trump to the presidency of the United States divided evangelicals on the role of both patriotism and nationalism in our churches. The rise of the Black Lives Matters movement divided evangelicals on the issue of racism and social justice. The imbalance of how Christians live out their beliefs in a culture increasingly veering away from their worldviews means evangelicals need guidance regarding their religious liberty.

It is the contention of this book that a preacher in nineteenth-century Victorian England can help in providing an ethic toward the vulnerable who struggle against the entrenched authorities of the present day. Spurgeon lived at a time when the philosophy of the government was "empire," a belief in the superiority of their culture over those they deemed savage and less sophisticated. For Christians like Spurgeon, this philosophy came against the Christian worldview that shows no partiality because all humans are image-bearers of God. Spurgeon used his platform to speak out against these issues while also displaying a love for his country.

Spurgeon also lived in a day when the political and the ecclesiastical were in full alliance. The head of the Church of England (Anglican Church) was also the reigning monarch over the British government. In the United States, many churches meld into the mindset and worldview of their preferred political party and, thus, use this as a test of faithfulness. Spurgeon saw the danger in these heavenly and earthly alliances. He spoke out frequently and fiercely against this problem.

Spurgeon's ministry coincided with changes in scientific trajectories and during a time when slavery in the American South was firmly entrenched. These matters, along with the established philosophy of "empire," developed a sense of racial superiority among the British that certainly influenced policy in society. London also received many refugees from Ireland, who suffered from the Irish Potato Famine of the 1840s and came to Great Britain to start a new life. Christians like Spurgeon preached against the religious and racial bigotry that the Irish faced at the hands of the Londoners. Spurgeon's biblical message reminded his countrymen that human beings are on equal footing as image-bearers of God.

This book analyzes the sermons of Charles Haddon Spurgeon to construct a gospel-centered ethic toward the vulnerable, specifically when addressing nationalism, racism, and religious liberty. Many of the events and situations that marked Spurgeon's day in the latter half of the nineteenth century parallel the events and situations of the present day. How Spurgeon approached them from his pulpit and pen will provide the present evangelical world with a needed template.

Finally, a special thanks to Drs. Michael McMullen and Owen Strachan, who guided me so well as my Ph.D. advisors at the Midwestern Baptist Theological Seminary. Also special thanks to Linda Stuchlik for her editorial expertise.

Introduction

If one attempts to construct an ethic, one must start with a fundamental question: What is an ethic? In the *Evangelical Dictionary of Theology*, the article on "Christian Ethical Systems" brings up a surprising deficiency throughout church history: "For generations Christians have found directions for daily life in the records of Jesus and the occasional counsels of the apostles; the church has never attempted to systemize its ethical teaching as it did its theology."[1] In another article from the same dictionary, White helped develop the definition for us further in an entry on "Biblical Ethics," which has, "its foundation in relationship with God; its objective, imposed obligation to obedience; its appeal to the deepest in people; its down-to-earth social relevance; and its capacity for continual adaptation and development."[2]

For the Christian, an ethic is an outworking of the portion of the Great Commandment where Christ tells the church to "love your neighbor as yourself" (Matt 22:39). How Christians act is grounded in what Christians believe regarding the work of God in the world and with them.

In searching and analyzing the sermons (along with the life and ministry) of Charles Haddon Spurgeon (1834–1892), this work seeks to construct a set of principles for evangelical Christians to use in caring for the vulnerable and downtrodden in society based on Spurgeon's sermons in fulfilling Christ's command to love one's neighbor. Spurgeon's doctrinal foundations grounded his ethics. What he believed about God's work in the world drove his actions in caring for those who bore the image of the One whom he trusted.

---

[1] White, "Christian Ethical Systems," *Evangelical Dictionary of Theology,* Second Edition, ed. Walter Elwell, 398.

[2] White, "Biblical Ethics," 402.

Spurgeon was easily the most influential evangelical of his day—an influence whose impact still carries into the contemporary evangelical world. For the sake of this work, the definition of "evangelical" for this work comes from David Bebbington, author of *Evangelicalism in Modern Britain: A History from the 1730s to the 1980s*, who breaks down this into four qualities: Conversionism (a transformation through being "born again" and a change of life), activism (expressing and demonstrating the gospel in mission and social reform efforts), biblicism (high regard for and obedience to the authority of the Bible), and crucicentrism (stress on the work of Christ on the cross in making the redemption of humanity possible). Spurgeon's paradigm matches Bebbington's definition.[3] The events and situations that marked Spurgeon's day in the latter half of the nineteenth century parallel the events and situations of the present day. How Spurgeon approached them from his pulpit and pen provides the current evangelical world with a template for constructing this ethic.

Introducing Charles Spurgeon

In his book, *The Saint and His Saviour*, Spurgeon wrote:

> Few men would dare to read their own autobiography if all their deeds were recorded in it; few can look back upon their entire career without a blush....Let yon heroic warrior of Jesus recount his deeds; but he, too, points to deep scars, the offspring of wounds received in the service of the evil one.[4]

Despite his fame, Spurgeon always recognized his vulnerability in both the physical and spiritual realms, which led Spurgeon to lean continually and fervently on the mercy and graciousness of Christ his Savior:

---

[3] David Bebbington, *Evangelicalism in Modern Britain: A History from the 1730s to the 1980s* (London: Unwin Hyman, 1989).

[4] Spurgeon, *The Saint and His Saviour,* 12; Quoted in Spurgeon, *Autobiography*, 1:2.

There are some houses in London which would tumble down if you were to remove those on either side that help to support them, but there are other houses which are self contained [*sic*]; you might pull all the houses in the parish down if you liked, but it would not hurt them. Now, the most of men in this world are like houses in a row, they lean one upon another, they are kept up by carnal comforts; but the Christian is self-sustained, and does not lean upon any arm of flesh....Is it not a blessed thing, dear friends, to have a heavenly constitution, a satisfaction which does not depend upon outward circumstances?[5]

Charles Spurgeon was born June 19, 1834, in Kelvedon, Essex to John and Eliza Spurgeon at a providential time in British history. He was the oldest of seventeen children, although only eight survived through infancy. When Spurgeon was eighteen months old, to ease the strain on his parents, he was moved to Stambourne to live with his grandparents James and Susannah Spurgeon until the age of seven. James was a pastor of a Congregational church for more than fifty years. Spurgeon treasured this time in his life because it allowed him to peruse his grandfather's impressive library, which was filled with formative Puritan volumes that would shape Spurgeon's theology for the rest of his life.

When Charles was ten, a visiting missionary named Richard Knill came to the Spurgeon household. Spurgeon noted, "In his heart burned the true missionary spirit, for he sought the souls of young and old, whenever they came in his way."[6] Knill spent a good amount of time with the young Spurgeon over the next three days, teaching and praying with him. Before Knill left, he placed Spurgeon on his knee and said, "This child will one day preach the gospel, and he will preach it to great multitudes. I am persuaded that he will preach in the chapel of Rowland Hill, where (I think he said) I am now the minister."[7] Knill's prophecy came to fruition, and thus made Spurgeon seek salvation even more since he "felt very

---

[5] Spurgeon, "The Happy Christian," *MTP* 13:176.

[6] Spurgeon, *Autobiography* 1:33.

[7] Spurgeon, *Autobiography* 1:34.

powerfully that no unconverted person might date to enter the ministry."[8]

Spurgeon was born just one year after the death of William Wilberforce (1759–1833), the man who spearheaded the abolitionist movement in the British Empire. Wilberforce's work and influence were not lost on Spurgeon or other evangelical believers of the day:

Long before, when England, free in every corner of it, yet held slaves in its colonies, it was God that gave Wilberforce, and raised him up to plead in Parliament the rights of men, till the command went forth—

"Thus saith Britannia, empress of the sea, —
Thy chains are broken; Africa, be free!'"

In all such acts of righteousness the coming forth of the man at the hour must be attributed to God's own hand.[9]

In another sermon in 1883 (fifty years after Wilberforce's death), Spurgeon invoked the spirit of Wilberforce again:

A healthy church kills error, and tears in pieces evil. Not so very long ago our nation tolerated slavery in our colonies. Philanthropists endeavoured to destroy slavery; but when was it utterly abolished? It was when Wilberforce roused the church of God, and when the church of God addressed herself to the conflict, then she tore the evil thing to pieces. I have been amused with what Wilberforce said the day after they passed the Act of Emancipation. He merrily said to a friend when it was all done, "Is there not something else we can abolish?" That was said playfully, but it shows the spirit of the church of God. She lives in conflict and victory; her mission is to destroy everything that is bad in the land.[10]

---

[8] Spurgeon, *Autobiography* 1:35.
[9] Spurgeon, "Certain Singular Subjects," *MTP* 29:1718 (1883).
[10] Spurgeon, "The Best War-Cry," *MTP* 29:1709 (1883).

The Christian conviction of Wilberforce fueled Spurgeon, for Wilberforce believed that God established the church to address evil in the culture and to serve as an instrument for its expulsion. This conviction set a trajectory in Spurgeon's life and work.

Spurgeon's conversion to Christianity was formative as well. Though raised in the Congregationalist denomination, his soul was vexed by the conviction of sin that would not loosen its grip. In his *Autobiography*, Spurgeon noted how in his young life he journeyed from chapel to chapel trying to find the answer to his question, "How can I get my sins forgiven?"

On January 6, 1850, a blizzard prevented Spurgeon from arriving at his intended destination by God's providence. The fifteen-year-old Spurgeon entered a small Primitive Methodist church on Artillery Street in Colchester, not only for the purpose of worship but also to find shelter from the brutal elements. The inclement weather prevented the regular minister from preaching that morning, so a layperson whom Spurgeon later described as "a shoemaker, or tailor, or something of that sort," went up into the pulpit to preach. He preached from Isaiah 45:22: "Look unto me, and be ye saved, all the ends of the earth."

Initially, Spurgeon struggled with this substitute preacher, believing him to be unskilled for the task of the morning. Spurgeon's initial assessment was blunter: "Now, it is well that preachers should be instructed, but this man was really stupid. He was obliged to stick to the text, for the simple reason that he had little else to say." He went on,

The preacher began thus, "My dear friends, this is a very simple text indeed. It says, 'Look.' Now lookin' don't take a deal of pain. It ain't liftin' your foot or your finger; it is just, "look." Well, a man needn't go to College to learn to look. You may be the biggest fool, and yet you can look. A man needn't be worth a thousand a year to be able to look. Anyone can look; even a child can look. But then the text says, 'Look unto *Me*.' Ay!" and he, in broad Essex, "many on ye are lookin' to yourselves, but it's no use lookin' there. You'll never find any comfort in yourselves. Some look to God the Father. No, look to him by-and-by, Jesus Christ says, 'Look unto *Me*.' Some on ye say, 'We must wait for the Spirit's working'.' You have no business with that just now. Look to *Christ*. The text says, 'Look unto *Me*.'"[11]

As he reached the end of his sermon, the preacher looked directly at Spurgeon and noted his misery, "You will always be miserable—miserable in life, and miserable in death,—if you don't obey my text; but if you obey now, this moment, you will be saved."[12] God used this preacher in all his vulnerability and unskilled state to show Spurgeon the way. He used this text and this truth many times after to lead others downtrodden in their sins to Christ.

As Spurgeon looked back on the event of his deliverance from sin, he never expressed a sense of entitlement to salvation; rather, he expressed great surprise that he could ever find the hope of forgiveness:

> I could not believe that it was possible that *my* sins could be forgiven. I do not know why, but I seemed to be the odd person in the world. When the catalogue was made out, it appeared to me that, for some reason, I must have been left out. If God had saved me, and not the world, I should have wondered indeed; but if He had saved all the world except me, that would have seemed to me to be but right. And now, being saved by grace, I cannot help saying, "I am indeed a brand plucked out of the fire!"[13]

Spurgeon experienced a needed vulnerability before God regarding his sin and brokenness. He could point not only to the Scriptures but to the gravity and joy of his own experience of justification, an experience he desired to see happen in others.

Ministry at Waterbeach

"Have you ever seen the poverty, and degradation, and misery of the inhabitants, and sighed over it…But was it ever your privilege to walk through that village again, in after years, when the gospel had

---

[11] Spurgeon, *Autobiography*, 1:87–88.
[12] Spurgeon, *Autobiography*, 1:88.
[13] Spurgeon, *Autobiography* 1:103.

been preached there? It has been mine."[14] Here, Spurgeon refers to the village of Waterbeach, located near Cambridge, approximately seventy miles northeast of London. Spurgeon first preached there on October 7, 1851, at the young age of seventeen and served as the town's pastor for two years. Even though this village was far away from the cultural center of England, the sight of God changing so many hardened sinners into followers of Christ confirmed God's call on his life and planted a seed of reliance on the gospel of his Lord.

He had no desire to climb the ecclesiastical ladder, as with other ministers in the more established Anglican church: "I would rather bring the poorest woman in the world to the feet of Jesus than I would be made Archbishop of Canterbury."[15] His heart always stayed with those who could offer little due to their social and economic status. Spurgeon's heart stayed with those forgotten communities, even to the point of urging younger preachers to take advantage of the opportunities they presented:

> Are there not other young men who might begin to speak for Jesus in some lowly fashion—young men who have hitherto been mute as fishes? Our villages and hamlets offer fine opportunities for youthful speakers…If they go out and tell from their hearts what the Lord has done for them, they will find ready listeners. Many of our young folks want to commence their service for Christ by doing great things or nothing at all; let none of my readers become victims of such an unreasonable ambition.[16]

Spurgeon refused to ignore those whom others disregarded or had forgotten; his advice is still serviceable to young, aspiring ministers in the twenty-first century. Even as Spurgeon moved to the historic New Park Street Church in London, the city could not diminish his love for those in the country.

---

[14] Spurgeon, *Autobiography*, 1:228.
[15] Spurgeon, *Autobiography,* 1:228.
[16] Spurgeon, *Autobiography,* 1:202.

How London Opened His Eyes
to the Vulnerable

In 1853, when London's New Park Street Chapel needed a new pastor, the deacons of the church approached Spurgeon in the hopes that he would accept the call. Attendance at New Park had declined, and they hoped a new pastor would lead them to better days. Still, the invitations surprised Spurgeon, considering the church's list of prestigious pastors such as Benjamin Keach, John Gill, and John Rippon.

For Spurgeon, the thought of leaving his beloved congregation grieved him greatly. Yet, he sensed God's call to leave Waterbeach for the big city of London—an intimidating prospect! In his acceptance letter, he confessed, "I sought not to come to you, for I was the minister of an obscure but affectionate people; I never solicited advancement. The first note of invitation from your deacons came quite unlooked-for, and I trembled at the idea of preaching in London."[17] Throughout his ministry, he referred to these two years at Waterbeach frequently and lovingly, serving as another example of how Spurgeon's heart bent toward those whom many had forgotten.

W.Y. Fullerton (1857–1932) penned a biography of Spurgeon from a vantage point that few possessed. Spurgeon befriended and mentored Fullerton (who came from Belfast) and would eventually become involved in Baptist work in London. In Chapter 4 of the biography ("Voice in the City"), Fullerton provides the reader with Spurgeon's impression of London as pastor of New Park Street Chapel in 1853:

> There were great areas of slums. It was estimated that over three thousand children under fourteen years of age were living as thieves and beggars; more than twenty thousand over fifteen years of age existed in idleness, and at least a hundred thousand were growing up without education. Ragged schools were even then places of peril to their teachers, and the common lodging houses sheltered tens of thousands "in lairs fitter to be the

---

[17] Spurgeon, *Autobiography,* 1:352.

habitation of hogs rather than of human beings." But people were beginning to care; Lord Shaftesbury was leading a crusade against the exploitation of the poor. It was a time of transition; the city was ready for a voice, and was not too large to be reached by it.[18]

Fullerton attested to the Christlike character and compassion of his mentor. Spurgeon could not ignore the plight of the children he encountered throughout the city streets, many of whom were migrants from Ireland during the Irish Famine of 1845–1852. This "holocaust," as one author described, led to the death of over one million people and another million fleeing from Ireland. Spurgeon likely saw this as an opportunity to meet a gospel need amid racism and immigration issues.[19]

In 1853, the first year of Spurgeon's tenure at New Park Street Chapel, cholera broke out in London due to unsanitary water, causing an outbreak of severe diarrhea and dehydration, which was highly contagious and often proved fatal. In 1857, Spurgeon wrote, "I remember, when the last time the cholera swept through your streets, ye hurried to your churches, and ye prayed; terror sat upon your countenances, and many of you cried aloud for deliverance. It came. What did you do? Alas! for your piety! It was as the morning cloud, as the early dew, it passed away."[20]

Even Spurgeon admitted to the terror he felt making pastoral visits to those in cholera's clutches. Store owners attached signs to their windows warning of the condition of the streets they occupied, urging pedestrians to travel a safer way. Yet, Spurgeon drew upon his calling to shepherd his flock, even in times such as this, including turning down many preaching and speaking engagements.[21] In an edition of his monthly magazine, *The Sword and the Trowel*, he spoke in the third person about what motivated him to press on in ministry during this potentially fatal era: "What is it that empowers yonder minister, in the midst of cholera, to climb up that creaking staircase and stand by the bed of some dying creature who has that

---

[18] Fullerton, *Charles Spurgeon: A Biography*, 52.
[19] Kinealy, *This Great Calamity: The Irish Famine 1845–52*.
[20] Spurgeon, "Fast Day Service," *NPSP* 3:386 (1857).
[21] *Autobiography* 1:372.

dire disease? It must be a thing of power that leads him to risk his life. It is the love of the Cross of Christ which bids him do it!"[22] For Spurgeon, the cross (which showed the suffering and vulnerability of Christ himself) fueled his compassion and care for those in such dire conditions.

During the COVID-19 pandemic of the twenty-first century, many pastors evaluated how to minister to those hurting during a time of sickness and quarantine. Spurgeon provides an example: He did not look to his pastoral status as a reason to avoid those affected. Rather, his calling as a pastor led him to serve as an under-shepherd of Christ's church in its times of distress and unrest.

Spurgeon's care for the downtrodden was not limited to his own country or countrymen. At times, he faulted his own country's imperial policies for creating societal problems. In 1857, colonial India rebelled, much to the shock and dismay of the English citizens. Spurgeon wondered if the gospel would have spread fast in India had it not been for the British Empire's colonization. He recounted that when a British officer became a Christian and asked to be baptized, the officer was then immediately stripped of his rank and sent home.

Spurgeon speculated whether greed had taken precedence over the gospel:

> Let the East India Company blush for ever [*sic*], he was stripped of his regimentals, dismissed the service and sent home, because he had become a Christian! Ah! we dreamed that if they had the power they would help us. Alas! the policy of greed cannot easily be made to assist the Kingdom of Christ.[23]

In another sermon, which gave blame to both sides, Spurgeon wondered if the rebellions might have turned out differently had England acted more like a "Christian nation."[24] Clearly, Spurgeon had no reservations about preaching truth to power, especially when that power was used to nullify the rights of the vulnerable.

---

[22] SS, 1:105. Quoted in Nettles, *Living by Revealed Truth: The Life and Pastoral Theology of Charles Haddon Spurgeon*, 78.

[23] Spurgeon, "The Independence of Christianity," *NPSP* 3:149 (1857).

[24] Spurgeon, "India's Ills and England's Sorrows," *NPSP* 3:150 (1857).

In 1864, Spurgeon referred to the political struggle of the Italian Unification in a sermon where he noted the "intolerable evil" of political tyranny. Spurgeon sought freedom for all to worship as their conscience dictated:

> Ye did well to crowd your streets and to welcome with your joyous acclamations the man who has broken the yoke from off the neck of the oppressed. Many sons of Italy have done valiantly, but he excels them all, and deserves the love of all the good and brave. Political slavery is an intolerable evil. To live, to think, to act, to speak, at the permission of another! Better have no life at all! To depend for my existence upon a despot's will is death itself.[25]

In the September 1869 issue of the *Sword and the Trowel*, Spurgeon reviewed James Greenwood's book, *The Seven Curses of London*. His purpose in reviewing this book was to "wish every Christian man could be made aware of the vice, the destitution and the misery which surround him; it would make him a better servant of the Lord. We are a vast deal too comfortable."[26] He commented on the seven curses, taking umbrage with how Greenwood dealt with the issues while overall appreciating the exposure provided to the church, sadly, was far too complacent to engage. The curses he listed were neglected children, professional thieves, professional gamblers, fallen women, drunkenness, betting gamblers, and the waste of charity. Though Spurgeon took issue with some of Greenwood's solutions; for instance, that the prostitution industry should be licensed, as well as Greenwood's penchant for taking prohibitionists lightly, Spurgeon used Greenwood's book because he sought to show his congregation and his readers the responsibility to engage in the plights of the culture, not to hide from the problems, but to springboard these contents to provide solutions fueled by the redemptive work of the gospel.

Spurgeon also took aim at another former British colony across the Atlantic, the United States, particularly the American

---

[25] Spurgeon, "The Great Liberator," *MTP* 10:565.

[26] Spurgeon, *The Sword and the Trowel*, September 1869, 385. Quoted in Nettles, *Living in Revealed Truth,* 109.

South, and their defense of slavery. Initially, newspapers on both sides of the ocean printed Spurgeon's sermons weekly, which not only edified those who read them but helped bring in a nice profit for the newspapers themselves. Yet, when Spurgeon expressed his hatred for American slavery, these newspapers and their readers in the American South began to push back. In the February 27, 1860 edition of the *Mississippi Free Trader*, he noted, "Finally, let me add that John Brown is immortal in the memories of good in England, and he lives in my heart as well."[27] Another article in the *Chicago Tribune* quoted Spurgeon's hatred for slavery from within his "inmost soul" to such a degree that he would not permit any "man stealer" to come to the Lord's Table for communion. Spurgeon's influence reached across the Atlantic and this quote's appearance in a Midwestern newspaper added fuel to the American fire.[28] Spurgeon showed his detestation for racism in any form, whether by plantation owners or the imperial government.

Providentially, Wilberforce lived long enough to see the passing of the Slavery Abolition Act, abolishing slavery in the British Empire. Wilberforce's influence extended to both British churches and politics alike. In his book, *A Practical View of Christianity* Wilberforce made the case for a Christianity that was socially conscience and, yes, practical:

> Is it not the great end of religion, and, in particular, the glory of Christianity, to extinguish the malignant passions; to curb the violence, to control the appetites, and to smooth the asperities of man; to make us compassionate and kind, and forgiving one to another; to make us good husbands, good fathers, good friends; and to render us active and useful in the discharge of the relative social and civil duties?[29]

Like Wilberforce, Spurgeon used his pulpit's influence at New Park Street Chapel and, later, Metropolitan Tabernacle to move hearts and minds toward helping the downtrodden. He penned this powerful sentiment in 1883:

---

[27] *Mississippi Free Trader*, 27 February 1860.
[28] "Spurgeon on Slavery," *Chicago Tribune*, Feb. 3, 1860.
[29] Wilberforce, *A Practical View of Christianity*, 179.

It seems to us that our Lord gave more prominence to cups of cold water, and garments made for the poor, and caring for little ones, that most people do nowadays. We would encourage our friends to attend to those humble, unobtrusive ministries which are seldom chronicled, and yet are essential to the success of the more manifest moral and spiritual work.[30]

Even at this stage in his ministry at the Metropolitan Tabernacle (where he served for thirty years), Spurgeon never lost his desire to reach out and care for others who had little, if anything, to give in return. Robyn Carswell rightly observed that Spurgeon had:

...drawn first blood [against his enemies] by preaching an uplifting message to the poor and lower classes; that they were not the rabble they had been told they were, but sons and daughters of the King of Heaven, to whom pedigrees and lineage mattered not.[31]

Spurgeon helped those who had been demoralized find hope and care in and through the gospel of Christ, from a place of his own physical and social struggles. The next section outlines several of his struggles, how he dealt with them, and how this helped him minister to others.

---

[30] Spurgeon, *The Sword and the Trowel,* August 1883.
[31] Carswell, "Charles Spurgeon: The Prince and the Paupers," *Historia* (2005), 126.

2

Interacting with Spurgeon Scholarship

While scholars have alluded to the areas of the vulnerable and downtrodden found in Spurgeon's ministry, such as the many organizations founded to help alleviate suffering, no dedicated written work exists that structures an ethic to help the vulnerable both inside and outside the church. In crafting an ethic of this nature, certain questions must be asked: how would Spurgeon address, for example, the immigration issue as one who loved his own country? Does Spurgeon's preaching address the pressing concern of many evangelicals over the loss of religious liberty at the hands of an overreaching government? The evangelical scholarly world needs to hear from Spurgeon regarding these areas.

This chapter seeks to examine significant works that address Spurgeon's aim and desire not only to preach the gospel but also to connect and engage with the vulnerable and downtrodden in society. These works address Spurgeon's theology, which was marked by his adherence to historic Calvinism, evangelicalism, the authority of Scripture, the condition of humanity regarding sin and the ailments that can afflict someone physically and mentally, and how these all played a part in how believers should treat each other and their vulnerable neighbor. While scores of scholars have interacted with Spurgeon regarding several subjects (showing the breadth of Spurgeon's ministry and influence), this work interacts with several scholars, while showing the need for work on an ethic toward the vulnerable heretofore unaddressed.

Biographies of Spurgeon

Arnold Dallimore's biography, *Spurgeon: The New Biography*, helped reintroduce Spurgeon's life and ministry to evangelicals in late twentieth-century North America. He notes how Spurgeon was a "typical Victorian Englishman. There was much that was good in society around him but also much that was evil. He devoted himself to one overwhelming task–the declaration of the life-transforming message of the gospel of Jesus Christ."[68] Dallimore (1911–1998) observed how Spurgeon, yes, recognized the prevalence of evil around him and sought to address those ills with his preaching ministry at Tabernacle. As mentioned in Chapter One, Dallimore's work brought the life and work of Spurgeon back into the American evangelical consciousness and provided a model for ministry that involved solid gospel preaching combined with a ministry to the downcast in society. When Dallimore's work arrived on the bookshelves in 1985, many influential evangelical denominations placed their trust almost exclusively in the political realm for Kingdom work to move forward. In contrast, Spurgeon's work did not rely on ingratiating himself with the governmental structures but sought to directly help those who could not help themselves.

Lewis Drummond's 836-page biography, *Spurgeon: Prince of Preachers*, was published less than a decade later after Dallimore's contribution. Drummond possessed a passion for evangelism and a longing to see the United States experience a spiritual awakening. His work with the Billy Graham Evangelistic Association, his fifteen-year tenure at the Southern Baptist Theological Seminary as professor of evangelism (1973–1988), followed by his presidency of the Southeastern Baptist Theological Seminary, all provided the Baptist and larger evangelical world with a scholarly ambition to make evangelism more prominent in these respective lanes.[69]

Drummond's work "picks up pithy poems, places, and personalities of [John] Bunyan's classic allegory and makes them the motif of Spurgeon's life and ministry."[70] The overall purpose of Drummond's work seeks to help the present generation understand the relevance of pilgrims (in reference to *Pilgrim's Progress* by Bunyan) journeying from the present world toward the world to

---

[68] Dallimore, *Spurgeon: The New Biography*, xvii.
[69] For a longer treatment of the life and work of Lewis Drummond: https://archives.sbts.edu/the-history-of-the-sbts/our-professors/lewis-drummond.
[70] Drummond, *Spurgeon: Prince of Preachers*, 13.

come. Drummond penned a chapter on "Spurgeon the Politician," which outlines his political philosophy and how he interacted in the pulpit with the various political issues of the day. Drummond's work was the first of its kind in this modern era to delve into Spurgeon's views on patriotism, nationalism, imperialism, war, and party politics. While this chapter will serve the thesis of this work in some helpful measure, Drummond did not provide an ethic from which succeeding generations could draw.

In the wake of Spurgeon's death, many friends and close associates penned biographies, giving future generations a perspective from men who possessed a front-row seat to his life and ministry. One such biographer, Charles Ray, penned a biography in the wake of Spurgeon's death simply entitled, *The Life of Charles Haddon Spurgeon.* One anecdote Ray passed along was Spurgeon's influence among the voters in an election for the Labor party candidates. Ray noted how one observer called him "the greatest single influence in South London in favor of Liberalism, upon whose every word thousands and thousands hang as if it were the very bread of life." [71] However, one should not conclude that Spurgeon was a liberal, politically nor theologically, for this was a comparative designation in political terms. He would vote whichever way aligned with his conservative theology in exhibiting Jesus' command to love our neighbor as ourselves, even if that landed him among what some would deem politically liberal.

Golden Pike's biography serves Spurgeon's scholarship well, given his relationship with Spurgeon and his capacity as an editor of *The Sword and the Trowel.* W.Y. Fullerton's *Charles Spurgeon: A Biography* (London: Williams and Norgate, 1920) stands as a first-hand account of Spurgeon's first impression upon arriving at London to pastor New Park Street Church in 1853. Fullerton (1857–1932), introduced in the first chapter, was a friend and protege of Spurgeon's from Belfast who would join the Kingdom work in London. Chapter Four of this work ("Voice in the City") shows the motivation behind Spurgeon's work in the city to alleviate many of its social ills. Fullerton's work aided greatly due to its lack of hagiography regarding his subject. Fullerton deals

---

[71] Ray, *The Life of Charles Haddon Spurgeon,* 386.

honestly with Spurgeon, readily showing both his faults and his positive traits.

Works about Personal Struggles

Spurgeon brought an authentic, gospel-centered ethic toward the vulnerable, with the operative word being *authentic*. Spurgeon struggled with several physical and mental maladies for most of his life. He described the pain he suffered from rheumatism and gout in his typical picturesque way: "Put your foot in a *vice* and turn the screw as tight as you can—that is *rheumatism*; give it an extra turn, and that is *rheumatic gout*."[72] Clearly, Spurgeon found ways to deal with the burdensome issues of not only rheumatism and gout, but also anxiety, depression[73], and Bright's disease (now diagnosed as lupus).[74]

Another work that addresses Spurgeon's physical and mental struggles is Zack Eswine's short work, *Spurgeon's Sorrows: Realistic Hope for Those Who Suffer from Depression*. Early in the work, Eswine shows Spurgeon's transparency regarding his depression soon after the tragedy at ten thousand seat Surrey Gardens Music Hall on Sunday, October 19, 1856. On that day, seven people died and many more were injured due to hooligans yelling "Fire!" (when there was no fire). This, along with the compounding criticism he received in the press, caused Spurgeon to sink into a deep depression that plagued him for the rest of his life. His transparency served to help others who received criticism from others. Eswine quotes Spurgeon's first sermon after the tragedy, preached on November 2, 1856:

> I almost regret this morning that I have ventured to occupy this pulpit, because I feel utterly unable to preach to you for your profit. I had thought that the quiet and repose of the last fortnight

---

[72] Fullerton, 125.

[73] Spurgeon, "Joy and Peace in Believing," *MTP* 12:692. "I am the subject of depressions of spirit so fearful that I hope none of you ever get to such extremes of wretchedness as I go to."

[74] Ort, "Sermon of the Week: No. 1099, The Man of Sorrows."

had removed the effects of that terrible catastrophe; but on coming back to the same spot again, and more especially, standing here to address you, I feel somewhat of those same painful emotions which well-nigh prostrated me before. You will therefore excuse me this morning ... I have been utterly unable to study... Oh, Spirit of God, magnify thy strength in thy servant's weakness, and enable him to honour his Lord, even when his soul is cast down within him.[75]

Eswine's short book (only 144 pages) seeks to help the reader see the book as "the handwritten note of one who wishes you well".[76] *Spurgeon's Sorrows* is dedicated to helping readers recognize that even though Spurgeon struggled with these serious issues, it did not disqualify God from using the maladies for His glory and purposes.

Peter Morden's works approach Spurgeon's life and work from several angles. Morden serves as a tutor in church history and spirituality at Spurgeon's College in London and as a member of the Baptist World Alliance Council. His beautifully illustrated biography, *C.H. Spurgeon: The People's Preacher*, interacts with some of the still shots from the documentary of the same name along with other period portraits and pictures from Spurgeon's life. David Coffey's Foreword to this work notes:

The need of the hour remains for there to be wisdom in the pulpit and compassion in the public square. Spurgeon serves as an outstanding mentor to preachers who want to set God's truth on fire and to all who desire to be salt and light Christians making a difference in God's world.[77]

Every biography of Spurgeon addresses his struggle with depression, which came in varying degrees after the Surrey Gardens tragedy and then with the advent of the numerous health problems that beset him. Morden verifies what this author believes about

---

[75] Spurgeon, "The Exaltation of Christ," *NPSP* 2:101 (1856). Quoted in Zack Eswine, *Spurgeon's Sorrows: Realistic Hope for Those Who Suffer from Depression,* Kindle location 154.

[76] Eswine, Kindle Location 194.

[77] Morden, *C.H. Spurgeon: The People's Preacher,* 7.

Spurgeon's ability and empathy to help others cope with their distress:

In this way Spurgeon learnt to find God in the midst of his distress. In fact he would testify that some of his closest times with his Lord were when he was in this state. His suffering also gave him great empathy with people who were going through difficulties of their own—those of his hearers who were coping with, say, illness or bereavement, or who were just struggling with the harshness of life in the grime and grind of Victorian London. Such people felt that here was a preacher who somehow understood what they themselves were going through.[78]

Morden delves into more detail in a subsequent journal article simply entitled "C.H. Spurgeon and Suffering," providing insight into Spurgeon's understanding and personal analysis of suffering:

Spurgeon came to believe that suffering resulted in important benefits for Christians, although for this to happen believers needed to remain faithful through their trials. The most important of these benefits was that believers could know closer communion with the suffering Christ as they experienced their own struggles.[79]

Morden seeks to show that suffering served a formative function in Spurgeon's life, even to the point of setting his content and tone in a way that benefited his listeners and readers. "Spurgeon's life and ministry provide a rich resource for those who are wrestling with the topic of suffering today."[80] Morden's article addresses the spirit of this paper in his theology of suffering, beginning with anthropology with the fall of man that brought the curse of sin and misery into the world. "There was a stress, then, on human responsibility for suffering, although Spurgeon also regarded its presence in the world

---

[78] Morden, *C.H. Spurgeon*, 83–84.
[79] Morden, "C.H. Spurgeon and Suffering," ERT (2011) 35:4, 307.
[80] Morden, "C.H. Spurgeon and Suffering," 307.

as being the result of the devil's activity."[81] Yet, Spurgeon's theology of suffering never fell outside divine sovereignty. Morden provides a helpful template for the responsibility of humanity and the work of Satan, underpinned by God's sovereignty:

> His focus on God's sovereignty provided an underpinning for his approach to questions of suffering, an approach in which he was able to maintain, firstly, that God was not to blame for "afflictions," which were the result of the fall; secondly, that God was still in control, being the sovereign "first cause" of suffering; and, thirdly, that God was still good, limiting the suffering of believers.[82]

Works about His Pastoral Ministry

When constructing an ethic from Spurgeon's preaching and writing, it is important to examine his pastoral ministry. These works are exceptional in their contribution to the field of Spurgeon scholarship. Tom Nettles penned a valuable work in said field with *Living by Revealed Truth: The Life and Pastoral Theology of Charles Haddon Spurgeon*. This work stands as one of the most authoritative and comprehensive works on Spurgeon in publication. Nettles provides a clear and definitive approach for the publishing of this work that reveals much about Spurgeon's heart for ministry. "The approach here involves an effort to suggest that Spurgeon, in every aspect of his ministry, was driven by a well-developed, clearly articulated systematic theology and by a commitment to a conversion ministry, both of which were conceived as consistent with revealed truth."[83] These commitments and convictions would be put to the test frequently, especially in the last chapter of Spurgeon's life during the Downgrade Controversy, leading to his resignation from the Baptist Union in 1888.

---

[81] Morden, "C.H. Spurgeon and Suffering," 311. Here, Morden comes to this conclusion from Spurgeon's sermon on 1 Peter 5:8–9, "The Roaring Lion," *MTP* 7:419 (1861).

[82] Morden, "C.H. Spurgeon and Suffering," 313.

[83] Nettles, *Living by Revealed Truth*, 12.

Chapter Five of Nettles' work ("Theological Method and Content") outlines three postulates of Spurgeon's biblical theology:

> His first postulate was, "He that cometh to God must believe that he is, and that he is a rewarder of them that diligently seek him." The second was, "He that believeth in God must accept Christ as mediator." The third continued, "He that accepteth the one mediator between God and men must receive the atonement." Any method that encourages less leaves a person with no reason to rejoice in God or sing praises to him with spirit and understanding.[84]

This theological method tethers Spurgeon to the authority and inspiration of Scripture, and how Christ's substitutionary atonement serves as mediator and intercessor for His people. This serves scholars well by providing a proper template for understanding Spurgeon's method of life and ministry: a desire to ground all in the Holy Writ of Scripture rather than in human systems. The temptation for those traveling in the evangelical lane is to embrace human systems and syncretize them with Scripture to provide a perceived relevance to the contemporary culture.

One last chapter in connection with Nettles' work (Chapter Ten) addresses the theological foundations for a benevolent ministry. Spurgeon, in life, ministry, and politics, sought to alleviate suffering and to aid those under oppression from the powers that be. Yet, Spurgeon's aim did not rest solely on the social justice that can often drift into a social gospel. Nettles puts the reader's mind to rest with this keen observation: "When benevolent work could be justified on the basis of the second great commandment alone, and should support all secular efforts at social betterment, the first great commandment combined with gospel knowledge justifies the involvement of a minister and a church in these activities."[85] This insight into Spurgeon's ministry ideally sets the table for the gospel-centered ethic toward the vulnerable which this paper will develop.

---

[84] Nettles, *Living by Revealed Truth*, 180.
[85] Nettles, *Living by Revealed Truth*, 342.

John Piper's series, *21 Servants of Sovereign Joy: Faithful, Flawed, and Fruitful,* identifies one of those servants as Spurgeon, devoting a chapter to Spurgeon's "Preaching Through Adversity." Piper introduces the chapter by showing the difference between pastoral work and other types of work, originally preached at the 1995 Bethlehem Conference for Pastors, that would eventually make up the contents of the aforementioned chapter:

> When a pastor's heart is breaking, therefore, he must labor with a broken instrument. Preaching is the pastor's main work, and preaching is heart work, not just mental work. The question becomes, then, not just how you keep living when the marriage is blank or when the finances don't reach or when the pews are bare and friends forsake you, but *How do you keep preaching?*[86]

Piper, in his unique turn of phrase, noted that, as a:

> ...maligned and suffering preacher [that] Spurgeon knew the everyday, homegrown variety of frustration and disappointment from lukewarm members... adversity to family pain ... unbelievable physical suffering [and] depression, [along with enduring] a lifetime of public ridicule and slander, sometimes of the more vicious kind.[87]

Piper concludes by demonstrating how Spurgeon preached through this severe adversity, relying on the sovereignty of God, engaging in the disciplines of prayer and meditation, taking seasons of rest, and leaning on his identity in Christ (rather than listening to man-made criticism). Though Piper's chapter in this collection is relatively short, he includes numerous quotes and insights that provide fodder for developing an ethic.

A Marvelous Ministry is a collection of essays by Tim Curnow, Erroll Hulse, David Kingdon, and Geoff Thomas. After the foundational introduction by Thomas, he also provides a brief biography in Chapter Two. In Chapter Three, Hulse addresses

---

[86] Piper, "Charles Spurgeon: Preaching Through Adversity," *21 Servants of Sovereign Joy: Faithful, Flawed, and Fruitful,* 747.

[87] Piper, "Charles Spurgeon," 756–60.

Spurgeon's practice of gospel invitation. Chapters Four through Five, by Kingdon, outline Spurgeon's social concern (Chapter Four) and the Downgrade Controversy (Chapter Five). Curnow concluded the collection in Chapter Six by discussing Spurgeon's activity in politics.

The benefit of this work is how Kingdon provides the harrowing statistics of Spurgeon's day, showing how disease and unsanitary conditions ran rampant through inner London.[88] Those employed worked in unsafe conditions and long hours, yet many poor were unemployed due to their lack of skills. Kingdon notes, "A dominant theme in Spurgeon's biblical social concern is sympathy. Himself a man of deep sympathy, moved to the depths of his being as he preached to sinners and ministered to the afflicted, he emphasized sympathy as a social concern."[89] This, along with Curnow's chapter on Spurgeon's political leanings, shows that Spurgeon sought to bring his conservative theology of being "salt and light" into every realm of society:

> Once Spurgeon achieved the pre-eminence as the most famous preacher in the land, he was consulted for his opinion on almost every issue of public concern. He became well-known as a Liberal supporter and it was not always easy for the public to draw a line between his role as pastor of the Tabernacle congregation and as a leading political Dissenter.[90]

Steve Miller's diminutive book, *C.H. Spurgeon on Spiritual Leadership*, devotes a chapter to this topic entitled, "A Heart for Service." The chapter begins:

---

[88] Edwin Chadwick in his *Report on the Sanitary Conditions of the Labouring Population* outlined in 1839 that those engaged in professions and their families died at the age of 45. Yet, the 273 tradesmen and their families lived and averaged a lifespan of 26 years; and the 1258 mechanics, servants and labourers and their families averaged an age of 16. *Modern English Society—History and Structure, 35.*

[89] Kingdon, "Spurgeon and his Social Concern," in Curnow, Hulse, Kingdon, and Thomas, *A Marvelous Ministry: How the All-round Ministry of Charles Haddon Spurgeon Speaks to us Today,* 99.

[90] Curnow, "Spurgeon's Politics," *A Marvelous Ministry,* 140.

Considering the magnitude of Charles Spurgeon's ministry and fame, it would have become very easy for him to become even marginally prideful about his accomplishments and assume an air of superiority over others. Yet no matter how much Spurgeon's successes and prominence continued to mount, he always wore the mantle of servant, maintaining a humility uncharacteristic of someone of his stature.[91]

In this small book, Miller shows the reader the many attributes of servanthood that Spurgeon possessed in his character (humility, kindness, selflessness, etc.).

Returning to Peter Morden, he converted his Ph.D. thesis into a book entitled *The Spirituality of Spurgeon: Communion with Christ and His People*. In Chapter 8, Morden addresses Spurgeon's activism, breaking up his activism into four periods of varying pace: 1850–53, 1854–66, 1867–79, and 1879–92. Yet his activism had "both evangelistic and social dimensions which were worked out through his preaching and pastoral ministry." [92] Morden also acknowledges Spurgeon's engagement in political expressions and opinions from the pulpit and in his writings in *The Sword and the Trowel*. Morden rightly notes that many biographies ignore Spurgeon's political activity (Drummond's biography notwithstanding), although a significant number of journal articles have filled this void with which this paper shall engage later. Yet, in specifically addressing Morden's book, he provides a helpful work but not one that cultivates and develops an ethic toward the vulnerable as culled from Spurgeon's sermons.

Morden connects with P.S. Kruppa's *Charles Haddon Spurgeon: A Preacher's Progress* and Albert R. Meredith's unpublished Ph.D. study *The Social and Political Views of C.H. Spurgeon, 1834–1892*. These works portray Spurgeon as a "prominent spokesman for political Dissent ... he played a significant part in helping to shape the politics of Nonconformity"[93]

---

[91] Miller, *C.H. Spurgeon on Leadership*, 74.

[92] Morden, *Communion with Christ and His People: The Spirituality of C.H. Spurgeon*, 199.

[93] Kruppa, *Charles Haddon Spurgeon: A Preacher's Progress*, 283. Quoted in Morden, *Communion with Christ,"* 196.

and, even further, "Politics and social issues were of central importance to Spurgeon,"[94] each of which Morden contends rightly that these "exaggerate the extent of Spurgeon's political activity."[95] Morden's work interacts with several other biographies and scholarly works that will contribute piece by piece in developing a needed ethic toward the vulnerable.

Mike Nicholls' 1994 contribution, *Lights to the World: History of Spurgeon's College, 1856–1992*, follows through on its title, giving a thorough account of the history of what Spurgeon called his "firstborn and best beloved."[96] Spurgeon's desire to reach all of England for Christ was partly represented by his church planting work. Nicholls noted that fifty-three of the sixty-two new London churches planted between 1865 and 1876 could be "attributed to Spurgeon's work," a legacy worth noting and remembering.[97] Spurgeon's leadership over his College, bringing to his students his experiences and convictions about pastoral ministry, was sufficiently passed on to his students who, it must be said, entered into the college already preaching and ministering (whether in churches or evangelistically in open air).

Horton Davies, professor of religion at Princeton University, penned a journal article on Spurgeon's expository preaching. In setting up the positives and negatives of expository preaching, Spurgeon is presented as a model example of both expository and evangelistic preaching (the latter making more use of topical textual preaching). Davies noted that, though Spurgeon never obtained a formal education, he was the epitome of self-education. Yet, Davies rightly noted, "No one could eliminate the artificialities of speech more readily than Spurgeon," providing two examples of how Spurgeon sought to preach as if "you were in your own houses" and to use phrases that would be heard in the market, should they serve

---

[94] Meredith, *The Social and Political Views of C.H. Spurgeon, 1834–1892*, 18.

[95] Morden, *Communion with Christ*, 196.

[96] Spurgeon, *Autobiography*, 3:137.

[97] Nicholls, *Lights to the World: History of Spurgeon's College, 1865–1992*, 98.

the user better.[98] His use of illustrations made Spurgeon "always understood, so concrete and usually commonplace were his illustrations, and rarely forgotten because of the humor and whimsicality of his speech."[99] Though Davies gives the reader examples to keep all who approach his sermons on their guard and thus lean away from hagiography, he gives credit to how Spurgeon accomplished much good in his preaching, especially in making the word accessible to the perceived non-intellectuals.[100]

Craig Skinner's article, simply titled "The Preaching of Charles Haddon Spurgeon," adds to that which Davies and others noted about Spurgeon's fresh, winsome style as opposed to the heavily rhetorical flourishes of his contemporaries. Skinner shows that Spurgeon sought to craft his sermons and deliveries so that all could understand and receive Christ:

> Through disciplining himself to adopt a precise, lucid, zestful, and sometimes colloquial style of thought and delivery, Spurgeon sought to sharpen the aptness of his presentations. He linked them clearly with his hearers' needs, using ideas phrased to arrest and hold their attention. Before congregations drowning in a maelstrom of sermonic words and ideas, he placed solid planks of biblical doctrine shaped to enable a firm grip from even the weakest in the faith.[101]

Though this work does not address Spurgeon's ministry, Christine Kinealy's *The Great Calamity: The Irish Famine 1845–52* speaks to the conditions Spurgeon found when he first came to London and the reasons behind those conditions. Fullerton's biography addressed Spurgeon's despondency in seeing the squalor

---

[98] Horton Davies, "Expository Preaching: Charles Haddon Spurgeon," *Foundations* 6 (1963), 19.

[99] Davies, "Expository Preaching," 20.

[100] Later in this paper, Kingdon (*A Marvelous Ministry,* 101) quotes Davies from another source (*Worship and Theology in England, Book 2: From Watts to Wesley to Martineau, 1690–1900,* 345) to dispute Davies' claim that "Spurgeon took the pietistical view that preachers should keep politics out of the pulpit."

[101] Skinner, "The Preaching of Charles Haddon Spurgeon," *Baptist History and Heritage,* 19:4.

in the British capital. Chapter One outlined how many of those who roamed the streets were migrants from Ireland during the Irish Famine of 1845. Kinealy referred to this time in Irish history as a "holocaust,"[102] which led to over one million people losing their lives and another one million fleeing Ireland. By 1861, approximately 600,000 Irish migrants lived in England. Up until that time, they faced racism and hatred due to their descent and their Roman Catholic religious beliefs, respectively. All over England, they lived in places of filth and squalor. Spurgeon likely saw this as an opportunity to meet a need amid racism and immigration issues.

Spurgeon also sought to extend his evangelistic work into France, as Ian Randall notes in his article, "C.H. Spurgeon: A Lover of France." Spurgeon's love for France began with his and Susannah's honeymoon in 1854. France also served as a place of convalescence from his numerous ailments, including his last when he died on January 31, 1892, with Susannah at his side. Randall's introduction to his article recalls "[Spurgeon's] relationship with France, his vision for evangelical advance among French-speaking people, his support of French Baptists and his finding a 'second home' in Mentone. It also shows some of his character traits and his concerns for the working classes."[103] Spurgeon's visits to Paris encouraged the struggling French Baptists, whom he found to be predominantly working class. Randall notes that Spurgeon believed that "the work of God was more long-lasting if it began among the poor."[104]

Of interest to Spurgeon scholars is an article from the February 3, 1860 edition of the *Chicago Tribune* which quoted Spurgeon on how he detested slavery from his "inmost soul" to such a degree that he would not permit any "man stealer" to come to the Lord's Table for communion. Spurgeon's influence had reached across the Atlantic, as evidenced by this quote appearing in this

---

[102] Kinealy, *This Great Calamity: The Irish Famine 1845–52*, Kindle location 118.

[103] Randall, "C.H. Spurgeon (1834–1892): A Lover of France," *EJT* 24:1(2015), 57.

[104] Spurgeon, "A Sabbath in Paris," *The Baptist Magazine*, February 1862, 85–89. Quoted in Randall, 61.

Midwestern United States newspaper added fuel to the American fire in dealing with the topic of slavery.[105]

In the next section, this work will examine authors who specifically addressed Spurgeon's theological convictions that spurred his ethic toward the downtrodden and vulnerable.

Works Outlining Spurgeon's Theological Convictions

Peter Morden again offers a helpful article on "C.H. Spurgeon and Prayer." Spurgeon's prayers in the corporate worship of the Metropolitan Tabernacle spoke volumes about his theological underpinnings. He continually laced the gospel throughout his prayers. Morden's reflection on the content of Spurgeon's prayers is most telling. He notes, "Christ and the atonement were central. Conversion came through regeneration (being 'lightened') which enabled sinners to look to the cross and receive salvation; but it was necessary to continue to look to the cross in confession, and thus receive forgiveness regularly."[106]

Spurgeon longed to see unbelievers come to Christ and believers strengthened in Christ. As a result, this practice of both verbal and unspoken intercession permeated his life and ministry. Morden observed that "whilst solitary prayer was important to him, he tends to stress the corporate. Most of all there was a resolute focus on Christ, particularly the crucified Christ, which was maintained across all the different dimensions of prayer we have examined."[107]

Robert Oliver's *History of the English Calvinistic Baptists, 1771–1892,* observes how Spurgeon's ministry descended from a long line of Calvinistic Baptists, not the least of which were Benjamin Keach, John Gill, and John Rippon, all of whom were previous pastors of the New Park Street Church before Spurgeon arrived in 1854. The year 1771 marked the death of John Gill. This year also saw two denominations emerge from English Separatism: the General Baptists of the Arminian theological bent; and the

---

[105] "Spurgeon on Slavery," *Chicago Tribune*, Feb. 3, 1860.

[106] Morden, "C.H. Spurgeon and Prayer," *Evangelical Quarterly* 84.4 (2012), 328.

[107] Morden, "Spurgeon and Prayer," 343.

Particular Baptists, which are Calvinist. The latter heeded the *1689 Confession of Faith* (a.k.a., the *Second London Confession*), a slightly edited version of the *Westminster Confession of Faith* (1647). Oliver's work ends in the year 1892, the year Spurgeon's life and ministry ended, and his faith was made sight.

Spurgeon ministered in the Free Church/Nonconformist tradition of Baptist life that owed much to the theology of John Calvin. Oliver noted that "so many of his critics, both Arminian and Hyper-Calvinist, were not familiar with the writings of Calvin or aware of the freeness with which he could present the gospel."[108] This shows that Spurgeon was no slave to a strawman system but conducted his own research past the prominent stereotypes of his day that extend even into contemporary times. Rather, Spurgeon saw the gospel reflected in Calvin's theology and sought to bring this gospel to all.

Sadly, toward the end of Spurgeon's life, the Downgrade Controversy moved the masses away from the primacy of doctrinal matters. Spurgeon saw his beloved denomination stray from the core tenets of faith and practice, such as leaving behind the authority of Scripture, the atoning work of Christ, and the eternal punishment of hell (to name a few). Spurgeon saw these deviations of the faith as contributing to the weakening of the churches and the trouble that ensued in the souls under their oversight. While the camps identified themselves with either Christian doctrine or Christian experience, Spurgeon saw these two side-by-side, working together. Oliver's work serves Spurgeon scholars well in showing how his Calvinism did not interfere with his gospel ministry.

Joel Gregory's journal article "Spurgeon's Resignation from the British Baptist Union: *A Microhistory of First Responders*" addressed the episodes that accelerated Spurgeon's death, mostly attributed to the Downgrade Controversy that happened toward the end of his life. His beloved Baptist Union began embracing heterodoxy. Gregory's article proves helpful in culling quotes from

---

[108] Oliver, *History of the English Calvinistic Baptists 1771–1892: From John Gill to C.H. Spurgeon* (Edinburgh, Scotland: Banner of Truth Trust, 2006), 345. "Commenting on 2 Peter 3:9, Calvin spoke of God's 'wondrous love to the human race, that he desires all men to be saved and is prepared to bring even the perishing to safety.'"

five articles in *The Sword and the Trowel* after Spurgeon resigned from the Baptist Union in 1888 and shows that Spurgeon was ready to stand up for orthodoxy and the protection of his churches against the powers seeking to undermine the truths of Scripture.[109]

Historian Gregory Wills provides an article showing Spurgeon's ecclesiology based on local church polity, Baptist denominationalism, and evangelical unity:

> Spurgeon's Baptist identity grew from his commitment to regeneration. He believed that believer's baptism and cooperation promoted regeneration. On this broad platform he participated in such Baptist organizations as the Baptist Union, the cooperative agency of British Particular and General Baptists roughly similar to the missionary conventions of the Southern and Northern Baptists of the same period. In 1888, Spurgeon resigned from the Baptist Union because the group tolerated modernist ministers in its membership. Modernism, Spurgeon believed, undermined regeneration. He altered his Baptist denominationalism to protect regeneration.[110]

Although Spurgeon was personally involved in Baptist work and his church belonged to the Baptist denomination, Wills points out that "the Baptist organizations needed him more than he needed them."[111] Regarding his church polity, he taught that the deacons "had [the] responsibility to care for the needs of the ministers, help the poor of the church, manage the church's property and finances, and provide for orderly worship." [112] As part of their many ministries, "the church engaged in benevolent activity on a remarkable scale. It established an orphanage and aided the poor in other ways." [113] Wills provides an excellent article regarding Spurgeon's views on his denominational and local church polity,

---

[109] Gregory, "Spurgeon's Resignation from the British Baptist Union: A Microhistory of First Responders," *Baptist History and Heritage* (Fall 2018).

[110] Wills, "The Ecclesiology of Charles H. Spurgeon: Unity, Orthodoxy, and Denominational Identity," *Baptist History and Heritage* (Autumn 1999), 70.

[111] Wills, "Ecclesiology," 70.

[112] Wills, "Ecclesiology," 67.

[113] Wills, "Ecclesiology," 71.

helpfully serving the cause of this work from an ecclesiastical polity standpoint.

Richard Day's work, *The Shadow of the Broad Brim,* further illustrates Spurgeon's comprehensive understanding of salvation that served as an amalgam of being chosen in Christ and giving a response to the free offer:

> Once, in Leeds, he read and commented on Romans 9 and 10. Reaching verse 10:13, he said: "Dear me, how wonderfully like John Wesley the apostle talked! 'Whosoever?' Why, that is a Methodist word, is it not?" (Amens from the Methodists; frowns from the Hypers!) "But (he proceeded) read verse 9:11 and see how wonderfully like John Calvin he (Paul) talked—' That the purpose of God according to election might stand.' (Amens and frowns change faces!) The fact is that the whole system of truth is neither here nor there. Be it ours to know what is scriptural in all systems, and accept it.[114]

Spurgeon's clear Calvinistic conviction did not mean he devoted himself to a camp, but to the Christ of Scripture.

Jerry Harmon's journal article "The Soteriology of Charles Haddon Spurgeon"[115] from Spring 2006 of the *Journal of Grace Evangelical Society* dissects the soteriology of Spurgeon as it pertains to his embracing of Calvinism paired with his offer of free grace to those who would believe. Harmon concludes that the evangelistic passion Spurgeon spread was due to his Reformed faith rather than despite it. This article helps the reader understand one of the motivations behind Spurgeon's preaching.

As alluded to earlier, Spurgeon had theological battles that show his convictions toward the vulnerable of the mind. Iain H. Murray's *Spurgeon V. Hyper-Calvinism: The Battle for Gospel Preaching* expounds on how Spurgeon's understanding of Calvinism put him at odds with fellow pastors and churches that held to what is known as Hyper-Calvinism. The latter disagreed with

---

[114] Day, *The Shadow of the Broad Brim,* 144. Quoted in Estep, "The Making of a Prophet: An Introduction to Charles Haddon Spurgeon," *Baptist History and Heritage* 19:4 (1984), 6.

[115] Jerry Harmon, "The Soteriology of Charles Spurgeon."

Spurgeon's free offer of the gospel, believing that God had already saved the elect without their response. As the subtitle indicates, Spurgeon believed that this was a battle for the gospel, calling this the "first serious attack on his preaching" in 1857.[116] Yet, Spurgeon felt the need by his examination of Scripture to provide the gospel to all. This serves the premise of this paper well, for if Spurgeon embraced and promoted the hyper-Calvinist bent, he would have neglected the free offer to the poor, vulnerable, and downtrodden. His preaching had no societal bounds.

David Nelson Duke contributes to Spurgeon scholarship with his 1987 article found in the *Baptist History and Heritage,* entitled "Charles Haddon Spurgeon: Social Concern Exceeding an Individualistic, Self-Help Ideology." Duke served as former president of William Jewell College in Liberty, Missouri. He noted that, during the Victorian era, three types of Christian social concern were on display: (1) individual charity, (2) reform, and (3) calls for changing the structure of society:

> Spurgeon fell in the first category, for he preached a message of individual regeneration. Yet despite this individualistic emphasis, his very conservative theology, his limited ecumenism, his resistance to modern thought, and his endorsement of the Victorian self-help ideology, he stands as a curious contrast to many of his evangelistic kinsmen then and now.[117]

This article provides insight into Spurgeon's social inclinations based on three pillars: (1) his call for absolute devotion to God in Christ; (2) his concern for the salvation of individual souls; and (3) his emphasis on Christian character which develops from the new nature found in Christ, though this article does move toward a more corporate sense of Christian life and ministry. Spurgeon's desire to see people come to Christ, engage with a body of local

---

[116] Murray, *Spurgeon V. Hyper-Calvinism: The Battle for Gospel Preaching,* 39.

[117] Duke, "Charles Haddon Spurgeon: Social Concern Exceeding an Individualistic, Self-Help Ideology." *Baptist History and Heritage, 22:4* (1987), 47.

believers, and a character to match played a role in how Spurgeon connected with the issues in the English culture of the day.[118]

Eric Hayden's book, *Spurgeon on Revival,* identifies how the social, moral, political, and spiritual culture of the late 1850s was in decline on both sides of the Atlantic. Prosperity, slavery, and indifference to the Christian message were prevalent. In 1857, revival (a.k.a., the Second Great Awakening) came to America, spreading to London two years later. These revivals were marked by united prayer that sprang up across the two countries. "Did [the revival] bring about any moral and social progress as well as spiritual blessing?"[119] Spurgeon's gauge of a Spirit-led revival lies in whether society has changed more toward the things of Christ and His good news. This work offers another piece into Spurgeon's evangelistic bent even as he embraced the doctrines of grace.

William Estep's article "The Making of a Prophet" discusses German Lutheran theologian Helmut Thielicke who connected "the nineteenth-century English Baptist minister Charles Haddon Spurgeon to a twentieth-century German Lutheran audience and subsequently to a contemporary English-speaking world which had almost forgotten 'the last of the Victorians.'"[120] Thielicke offers his belief on Spurgeon's influence in nineteenth-century England:

Yet the secret of Spurgeon's greatness and immense popularity was not in his voice, use of the English language, nor humor. Doubtless it was a combination of many factors, among which were the following: (1) Spurgeon was utterly sincere.... (2) He had complete confidence in the gospel.... (3) Money had no attraction for Spurgeon. He gave away a fortune. At his death there was little left other than enough to care for his widow. (4) Above all else Spurgeon had an unshakable confidence in God.[121]

---

[118] Ibid., 47.

[119] Hayden, *Spurgeon on Revival,* 57.

[120] Estep, "The Making of a Prophet: An Introduction to Charles Haddon Spurgeon," *Baptist History and Heritage,* 19:4 (1984), 3.

[121] Estep, "The Making of a Prophet," 14.

Donald H. Ashmall's article on the spiritual development in the free church tradition addresses the "exercises and attitudes which relate to the perception and understanding of the individual Christian," and how it interacts with Spurgeon's "strain of modified Calvinism which was dominant among the free churches during the latter part of the nineteenth century."[122] This article opens the door to seeing how Spurgeon's theological views played a part in his views on nationalism and other social issues of the day. This subject contributes to Spurgeon's ethic toward the vulnerable in showing how a strict patriotic/nationalistic view, especially in Spurgeon's context of the British empire, could be leveraged into a racial or societal superiority over other people and could counter Christ's command of "love your neighbor" (Mt 5:44; 22:37).

Duncan Ferguson gives Spurgeon scholarship another boost in his article, "The Bible and Protestant Orthodoxy: The Hermeneutics of Charles Spurgeon." Ferguson observed that Spurgeon was "a nineteenth-century representative of Protestant orthodoxy, and more particularly of the Puritans."[123] What is more,

> The Bible was inspired and authoritative. God was sovereign in creation, providence and redemption. Christ the Son of God was sinful mankind's substitute in his atoning sacrifice at Calvary, and human beings are justified by faith in this deed. The Holy Spirit is active in the lives of the saints, guiding them in holy living, and ultimately, they will persevere until the return of Christ. These mutually dependent Puritan assumptions that Spurgeon adopted constitute the major influence on his interpretation of Scripture. Taken as a whole they tend toward being a comprehensive world view and function consistently, consciously and rationally throughout his hermeneutical system.[124]

---

[122] Ashmall, "Spiritual Development and the Free Church Tradition: The Inner Pilgrimage," *Andover Newton Quarterly 20* (1980), 141.

[123] Ferguson, "The Bible and Protestant Orthodoxy: The Hermeneutics of Charles Spurgeon," *Journal of the Evangelical Theological Society* 25:4 (December 1982), 457.

[124] Ibid., 459.

Elijah Hixson's contribution, "New Testament Textual Criticism in the Ministry of Charles Haddon Spurgeon," discusses Spurgeon's view of the textual criticism arguments that prevailed in the late nineteenth century, underlying Spurgeon's view was that translations be faithful to the original languages (Hebrew and Greek):

> This article seeks to understand better how Spurgeon used NT textual criticism in his ministry and to present Spurgeon as a model for contemporary ministers and scholars through an analysis of his remarks on textual variants and critical editions of the NT. An examination of Spurgeon's works reveals that, although he lived in an age dominated by the King James, or Authorized Version (AV), he was aware of variant readings in the NT manuscripts.[125]

Though Spurgeon enjoyed and profited from the scholarly aspect of the subject of textual criticism, he did not want his deep study to be a stumbling block for his flock.[126] While Hixson believes that Spurgeon did not delve deeply into this issue and wonders if Spurgeon had much to contribute, Spurgeon contributed what he deemed necessary as a pastor of a local church.

David Bebbington's seminal work, *Evangelicalism in Modern Britain: A History from the 1730s to the 1980s*, fits Spurgeon's life and ministry into the context of British Protestant history. This evangelical movement, spearheaded toward the end by Spurgeon, helped transform the landscape of England into a place where the gospel held sway. Toward the end of Spurgeon's life, the tide had turned as the culture began to influence the evangelical

---

[125] Hixson, "New Testament Textual Criticism in the Ministry of Charles Haddon Spurgeon," *Journal of the Evangelical Theological Society* 57/3 (2014), 556.

[126] Hixson early on quotes Spurgeon, "On Commenting," in *Commenting and Commentaries*, 31. "*Do not needlessly amend our authorised version.* It is faulty in many places, but still it is a grand work taking it for all in all, and it is unwise to be making every old lady distrust the only Bible she can get at, or what is more likely, mistrust you for falling out with her cherished treasure. Correct where correction must be for truth's sake, but never for the vainglorious display of your critical ability."

movement, but Spurgeon still held enough influence to prevent the movement from cracking altogether.

Christian George's extensive journal article on "An analysis of the doctrine of the priesthood of Jesus Christ in the functional Christology of Charles Haddon Spurgeon," derived from his doctoral dissertation[127], provides a needed avenue of understanding Spurgeon's views on Christ as mediator, sacrifice, intercessor, and advocate. In developing a gospel-centered ethic, Spurgeon's theology plays prominently. George's contribution in analyzing his Christology is seen early in developing a Christology "'from below' in which Christ's humanity becomes the starting point for discussing his priestly duties."[128]

> He then includes a quote that directly pertains to what this paper seeks to accomplish: He [Christ] must needs sit down and hear all the trembling petitions of troubled mothers who had come from the utmost end of Israel laden with their domestic burdens; he must listen to all the complaints of the oppressed, the woes of the afflicted, the trials of the poor, the perplexities of the distracted; and then, as a man of God, he was ordained to take all these things in prayer before the Most High.[129]

The mediatorial and intercessory work of Christ as our Great High Priest includes all who trust in the word and work of Christ, regardless of their financial or societal status.

Phillip Ort, former curator of The Spurgeon Library at Midwestern Baptist Theological Seminary in Kansas City, Missouri, along with Timothy Gatewood and Edward Romine, interact with Bebbington's work in a recent article, *Evangelicalism in Modern Britain: A History from the 1730s to the 1980s*. These authors identify the importance of Bebbington's work in identifying four

---

[127] George, "Jesus Christ, The 'Prince of Pilgrims': A Critical Analysis of the Ontological, Functional, and Exegetical Christologies in the Sermons, Writings, and Lectures of Charles Haddon Spurgeon (1834–1892)."

[128] George, "An analysis of the doctrine of the priesthood of Jesus Christ in the functional Christology of Charles Haddon Spurgeon," *Theology in Scotland* (2011), 36.

[129] Spurgeon, "The Tenderness of Jesus," *MTP* 36:315 (1890).

key convictions of evangelicalism: Conversionism, activism, Biblicism, and Crucicentrism. The article zeroes in on how Charles Spurgeon is the epitome of an evangelical, fleshing out Spurgeon's ministry through the paradigm of these key convictions.[130]

Nathan Rose, Ph.D. graduate from Midwestern Baptist Theological Seminary in Kansas City, Missouri, shows in his article "Spurgeon and the Slavery Controversy of 1860: A Critical Analysis of the Anthropology of Charles Haddon Spurgeon, as it relates specifically to his Stance on Slavery" that Spurgeon's stance on slavery brought on a visceral and vitriolic reaction from newspapers in the American South:

> Spurgeon despised slavery and its advocates because the practice contradicted his understanding of Scripture. The Bible taught him that every person, regardless of his or her race or class, was a human being made in the image of God and was worthy of honor and respect. [131]

Some newspaper editors redacted the offending parts, while others refused to carry his sermons altogether. Rose notes that Spurgeon's anthropology regarding the *Imago Dei*, the fall of man, and the need for the rescuing work of the gospel is what fueled his view of slavery and other forms of societal injustice.[132] Spurgeon's theology spurred on his desire to help society's reforms, all the while giving glory to God who changes hearts and minds. The society in which Spurgeon preached somewhat resonated with these theological views, but Spurgeon always kept these before his people and the city in which he ministered.

---

[130] Ort, Gatewood, and Romine, "Charles Spurgeon: The Quintessential Evangelical," *Midwestern Journal of Theology* 18:1 (2019): 104–125.

[131] Rose, "Spurgeon and the Slavery Controversy of 1860: A Critical Analysis of the Anthropology of Charles Haddon Spurgeon, as it relates specifically to his Stance on Slavery," *Midwestern Journal of Theology*: 16:1 (2017): 20–37.

[132] Rose, "Spurgeon and the Slavery Controversy of 1860," 20–37.

Conclusion

Even though Spurgeon died 130 years ago (1892), his life and ministry continue to influence evangelicals today whether or not they are aware of it. Analysis and construction of a gospel-centered ethic were aided by the scholarship previously outlined. Many have penned works and journal articles outlining Spurgeon's theology, pastoral work, and personal struggles.

In summarizing the previously attributed works above, one can deduce that Spurgeon, while never wishing his personal physical, mental, and emotional maladies on another person, was grateful for these for one simple reason: he was pushed to rely more fully on Christ. As a result, his transparency aided others who experienced similar struggles. He never put on airs to hide his grappling with pain. Though his sicknesses never served as the focus nor were leveraged for personal sympathy, he was honest with his people and to those outside the church by virtue of the publication of his sermons on both sides of the Atlantic, and through his magazine *The Sword and the Trowel*, as well.

Spurgeon's theological convictions upheld his personal struggles because of his view of the authority of Scripture, the sovereignty of God, the efficacy of Christ's work on the cross, and the concern for those in his church and city. His embracing of Puritan theology steered his conviction toward Calvinism, not to be confused with the hyper-Calvinism of the day. As a Calvinist, Spurgeon went against the strawmen his opponents set up to represent him by trusting in God to save but also by calling for a response for salvation during his sermons. With this, everything he accomplished was laced with prayer, which was especially needed during the last chapter of his life during the Downgrade Controversy, where he left his beloved Baptist Union in 1888 (a mere four years before his death).

His work in ministry could be boiled down to the Great Commandment of loving God completely and loving thy neighbor sacrificially. From his tenure as pastor at Waterbeach to the moment he set foot in London, the poor and vulnerable gripped his mind and heart with a desire not only to tell them about the Good News of Christ but to help alleviate the suffering that gripped them. Spurgeon did not rely on social engagement as the primary means to help the vulnerable of society, and he did not lean on doctrine at the expense of Christian experience and obedience. Spurgeon saw that the gospel of Christ led to an outward and active expression of love for those who struggled most.

What is notably missing in extended treatments of Spurgeon's life and ministry is his addressing of the topics of patriotism, nationalism, racism, and religious liberty, though each of these topics contributes to the overall construction of a gospel-centered ethic toward the vulnerable. This work aims to fill that void in Spurgeon's scholarship.

3

In Relation to Nationalism and Imperialism in Great Britain

Charles Spurgeon saw himself as a dual citizen—a citizen of the Empire of Great Britain and a citizen of heaven. Yet, whenever both came into conflict, the primary citizenship was the heavenly one that Christ secured on his behalf. In an 1880 sermon on Colossians 3:1–2, Spurgeon drove home how, due to the resurrection of Christ, no other home must exist outside the heavenly home purchased for us. "Now, beloved, you are new creatures, the produce of a second birth, begotten again in Christ Jesus unto newness of life. Christ is your life; such a life as you never knew before, nor could have known apart from him. If ye then be risen with Christ ye walk in newness of life, while the world abideth in death."[133]

What does this world offer? In the same sermon, Spurgeon proclaimed the rescuing work of Christ:

> There was corruption in our mind and it was working irresistibly towards every evil and offensive thing. In many the corruption did not appear upon the surface, but it worked within; in others it was conspicuous and fearful to look upon. How great the change! For now the power of corruption within us is broken, the new life has overcome.[134]

Though followers of Christ occupy the sociopolitical landscape alongside those who refused to follow Christ by choosing other religious paths, Spurgeon believed that the Christian's status as a citizen of heaven would aid their earthly citizenship. Their belief

---

[133] Spurgeon, "Following the Risen Christ," *MTP* 26 (1880).
[134] Spurgeon, "Following the Risen Christ."

stoked the fire of a life that would benefit all in honoring God and loving their neighbor.

This chapter examines the preaching of Spurgeon in relation to nationalism, patriotism, and (in the case of Spurgeon) imperialism and creates an ethic to aid twenty-first-century evangelicals navigating through nationalistic and patriotic tendencies found in churches. Spurgeon's preaching can be condensed into four key ideas: (1) A Christian's primary citizenship is in heaven; (2) a Christian's secondary citizenship is with whom an earthly allegiance is sworn as citizens of a country; (3) Christians must beware of mixing Christianity with politics; (4) while geopolitical borders exist in which governments defend and protect the citizenry within said borders, Christianity has no sociopolitical borders.

A Christian's Primary
Citizenship is in Heaven

To Charles Haddon Spurgeon, any Christian whose nationalism or patriotism usurped the primary citizenship of heaven should repent. "I cannot say that I delight in political Christians; I fear that party-strife is a serious trial to believers, and I cannot reconcile our heavenly citizenship with the schemes of the hustlings and the riot of the polling-booth."[135]

Yes, Spurgeon was a patriot; he was loyal to the Crown and his beloved Britain, remained politically active in his support of the Labor Party, and expressed his political leanings in his sermons and writings. But Spurgeon's political leaning was not in blind loyalty, for the heavenly citizenship took precedence (for to Spurgeon, Christ was the true Crown). In a lecture to his students at the Pastors' College, he urged them to focus on one main task, which was not politics: "Soul winning is the chief business of the Christian minister; indeed, it should be the main pursuit of every true believer."[136]

Spurgeon held firmly to Philippians 3:20–21, where the apostle Paul reminded the church at Philippi, "But our citizenship is

---

[135] Spurgeon, "Citizenship in Heaven," *MTP* 8:476 (1862).
[136] Spurgeon, S&T, November 1879, front page.

in heaven, and from it we await a Savior, the Lord Jesus Christ, who will transform our lowly body to be like his glorious body." In an 1874 sermon on this text, Spurgeon observed, "It is a greater honour to serve Christ in the most menial capacity than to occupy the thrones of the Caesars." [137] Christians recognize what awaits, allowing them to approach any task placed before them with joy as strangers and sojourners in this world. Those who make their home in their respective cultures seek to find their ultimate hope and identity in the transient nature of this creation, only to realize in the end the foolishness of their striving:

> You believe that while you are living here it is a good thing to make the best you can of it, and that then you will die and be buried, and there will be an end of you! What a poor, miserable, ignorant belief this is! But when you believe in what God reveals, and come to walk by faith, how your information expands! Now, riddles are all unriddled, and enigmas are all solved, and now you begin to comprehend things in a way which you never could have done had you walked only by sight.[138]

Given that Christians' citizenships stand in heaven, even as they live on the earth, walking by faith and not by sight (see 2 Cor 5:7), they watch for the One whom they do not see and serve the One who has called them with a voice they have never heard, and whose heart beats for a place where they have never resided. In an 1862 sermon, Spurgeon reminded his congregation of the content of their conversation as citizens of heaven:

> By the honourable citizenship which has been bestowed upon you, I shall beseech you to let your conversation be in heaven, and I shall urge that most prevailing argument, that the Lord Jesus Christ cometh, and therefore we should be as men that watch for our Lord, diligently doing service unto Him, that when He cometh he may say unto us, "Well done, good and faithful servants."[139]

---

[137] Spurgeon, "All for Jesus," *MTP* 20:1205 (1874).
[138] Spurgeon, "Faith versus Sight," *MTP* 12:677 (1866).
[139] Spurgeon, "Citizenship in Heaven," *MTP* 8:476 (1862).

Spurgeon never denied the legitimacy of the earthly citizenships that Christians hold. In commenting on Queen Victoria's Jubilee ceremony in 1887, Spurgeon took time to pronounce "God save the Queen!" and express thankfulness for such a benevolent ruler. Here, Spurgeon demonstrated to his congregation and to all who would come in succeeding generations that showing gratitude to God for a benevolent earthly ruler is permissible. "Let us take care to blend a holy gratitude to God with our fervent patriotism. Be it ours to praise and bless the God who has sent us these favors."[140] Yet, he would always remind them of their citizenship in heaven:

But, brethren, let us learn from the citizens of an earthly kingdom to rejoice in our heavenly King. Let us elevate our fervour into the higher sphere. There is another King, one Jesus; and, as believers in him, we are more truly citizens of the heavenly Jerusalem than of any city or country upon earth. Our divine Lord has called out believers from among the sons of men to make them a peculiar people, a nation set apart unto himself.[141]

In 1857 (as alluded to in Chapter One), India rebelled against England in a colonial mutiny, which was a national embarrassment. Spurgeon minced no words: "The government of India has been a cruel government; it has much for which to appear before the bar of God. It's tortures—if the best evidence is to be believed—have been of the most inhuman kind." Also, in 1864 Spurgeon referred to the political struggle of the Italian Unification, in which he noted, "Political slavery is an intolerable evil. To live, to think, to act, to speak, at the permissions of another! Better to have no life at all!"[142] Spurgeon also held strong convictions about the systemic slavery prevalent in the American South, which will be addressed more fully later in this work. While the power wielded by these empires, "despots" and slave masters may impress some looking in from the

---

[140] Spurgeon, "Jubilee Joy; or, Believers Joyful in Their King," *MTP* 33:1968 (1887).

[141] Spurgeon, "Jubilee Joy."

[142] Spurgeon, "The Great Liberator," *MTP* 10:565 (1864).

outside, Spurgeon's interest lay with how Christ looked on such use of influence. When regarding the Roman Empire, one such undeniably influential empire, Spurgeon stated:

> I do not find the Redeemer marvelled at the force and majesty of the Roman empire, and yet it wielded a very remarkable power, an all-pervading and irresistible influence. Out of utter insignificance the Roman empire had developed itself into a universal monarchy which locked the entire world in its embrace of iron. Scarce a dog dared move his tongue without the leave of Cæsar. In every place, whether sacred or profane, the insignia of the empire were conspicuous; in every nation, whether polite or barbarous, the tramp of the imperial legionaries was heard; and the eagles of Rome were fluttering on every hill and in every dale; and yet I do not find that Jesus ever marvelled at all the pomp and energy of the rule of the Caesars.[143]

Like Rome, England used its influence to intimidate its colonies to submit to its unquestioned rule. Spurgeon saw many historical examples of this "all-pervading and irresistible influence"[144] that provided necessary lessons moving forward.

The Italian authorities of the Italian Unification sought to keep the people under the thumb of their rulers. In the United States, specifically in the Confederate States of America (a.k.a, the American South), where the slave masters and, once the Confederacy seceded, the American Southern government sought to keep their economic status intact by more stringently affirming the practice of the peculiar institution.[145] The pomp and glory, whether

---

[143] Spurgeon, "The Sad Wonder," *MTP* 16:935 (1870).

[144] Spurgeon, "The Sad Wonder."

[145] "Constitution of the Confederate States, March 11, 1861. cdli:wiki http://avalon.law.yale.edu/19th_century/csa_csa.asp. The clarity of Article IV, Section 3, Paragraph 3 of their constitution is indisputable proof that the American South seceded over the issue of slavery. "The Confederate States may acquire new territory; and Congress shall have power to legislate and provide governments for the inhabitants of all territory belonging to the Confederate States, lying without the limits of the several States; and may permit them, at such times, and in such manner as may by law provide, to form States to be admitted to the Confederacy. In all such territory the institution of negro slavery, as it now exists in the

found in the monarch's palace of England, in Italy, or in the plantations of the American South, existed as a tragedy in Spurgeon's eyes and, according to Spurgeon, did not impress Jesus in the least.

The foundational concern for Spurgeon was grounded in how England's tyrannical behavior worldwide stood in stark contrast to the rich heritage of Christianity—as well as having the monarch of England serve as the head of the state church. While this chapter will delve into this area in more detail later, Spurgeon rightly saw the problem in mixing the spiritual realm with the earthly realm, the heavenly and earthly citizenship melded into one worldview and authoritarian system. Spurgeon echoed the New Testament trajectory by preaching and writing about how these two realms must remain separate, with the heavenly citizenship influencing the earthly one.

Before moving on to the next section, take one more reminder that Spurgeon, while patriotic and loyal to the crown, used the royal family in a sermon on Psalm 2 to remind his clergy that there is but one King that transcends the ages:

Why look at Englishmen, how they spring to their feet and sing with enthusiasm—

"God save our gracious Queen,
Long live our noble Queen,
God save the Queen!"

And is it a hard thing for you and me to be bidden to cry, "God save King Jesus! Spread his kingdom! Let him reign, King of kings and Lord of lords I Let him reign in our hearts?" Is it a hard thing to bow before his gentle scepter? Is there any cruelty in the demand, that we should submit ourselves to the law of right, and rectitude, and justice, and love?[146]

Confederate States, shall be recognized and protected by Congress and by the Territorial government; and the inhabitants of the several Confederate States and Territories shall have the right to take to such Territory any slaves lawfully held by them in any of the States or Territories of the Confederate States."

[146] Spurgeon, "An Earnest Invitation," *MTP* 5:260 (1859).

Christians are Still Citizens of
Their Respective Earthly Kingdoms

Spurgeon's conviction regarding the Christian's primary citizenship standing firm in heaven did not diminish the responsibility of Christians in their earthly allegiance as citizens of their respective countries. Spurgeon believed that God had his benevolent hand on Queen Victoria in bringing her from the despotism of previous monarchs to religious liberty based on Scripture. In 1855, in a very early sermon in his New Park Street Chapel ministry, he preached,

> This land is the home of liberty. But why is it so? I take it, it is not so much because of our institutions as because the Spirit of the Lord is here—the spirit of true and hearty religion. There was a time, remember, when England was no more free than any other country, when men could not speak their sentiments freely, when kings were despots, when Parliaments were but a name. Who won our liberties for us? Who have loosed our chains? Under the hand of God, I say, the men of religion—men like the great and glorious Cromwell, who would have liberty of conscience, or die—men who, if they could not reach kings' hearts, because they were unsearchable in cunning, would strike kings low, rather than they would be slaves. We owe our liberty to men of religion, to men of the stern Puritanical school—men who scorned to play the craven and yield their principles at the command of man. And if we ever are to maintain our liberty (as God grant we may) it shall be kept in England by religious liberty—by religion. This Bible is the Magna Charta of old Britain.[147]

Spurgeon certainly believed that the greatness of Great Britain derived from the stand they took as a Christian nation. His sentiment echoes many who express the same line of thought regarding God "shedding His grace"[148] on America, a country grounded in a mixture of biblical and Enlightenment principles.

---

[147] Spurgeon, "Spiritual Liberty," *MTP* 1:9 (1855).
[148] Bates, "America, the Beautiful."

Debates surrounding Oliver Cromwell (1599–1658) in England and the Founding Fathers in America who secured religious freedoms will continue (and will be addressed later in this work).

Spurgeon viewed the right and privilege of voting as gifts that came with citizenship. Thus, Christians should spend time researching the platforms of the candidates and voting according to Christian principles, not merely according to party loyalty. "Every God-fearing man should give his vote with as much devotion as he prays."[149] For Spurgeon, this was no mere hyperbole—this reflected his conviction of being a citizen both of heaven (prayer) and of earth (voting). Granted, Spurgeon's concern lay with his congregation, not with the worldwide masses who read his published sermons while living in a non-democratic society. Yet, the underlying principle transfers to any governmental structure—engage in whatever process is possible, always bathed in prayer.

Spurgeon's theological leanings fueled his political stance, making him difficult to pin on political issues. Baptist historian William Estep, one of many who controversially claimed Spurgeon as a political liberal, noted, "He lent his support to the fledgling labor movement, persuading members of his church to contribute to the relief of the striking workers who were struggling to survive."[150] Again, Spurgeon's conservative theology leaned into Christ's command of loving one's neighbor as oneself, which, in turn, influenced his politics. While Spurgeon sought out candidates to vote into office who led with Christian principles, he also took the initiative to open ministries to help alleviate societal suffering via his church and personally; such as orphanages, nursing homes, and schools, and providing books for preachers who could not afford them. Though engaged in the political process, Spurgeon did not expect the government to provide every possible service. Spurgeon felt if the church could help, he would procure the resources necessary to meet the need.

Spurgeon also believed that, as Christians who lived as earthly citizens of earthly kingdoms and republics, they must pray

---

[149] Burley, *Spurgeon and His Friendships* (Norwich, England: Epworth Press, 1933), 128.

[150] Estep, "The Making of a Prophet," 11.

for their respective leaders, as commanded in 1 Timothy 2:1–4. In an 1859 sermon, Spurgeon showed from the Scriptures the gravity leaders have in their responsibility to their citizens and, ultimately, to God.

> There is a weighing time for kings and emperors, and all the monarchs of the earth, albeit some of them have exalted themselves to a position in which they appear to be irresponsible to man. Though they escape the scales on earth, they must surely be tried at the bar of God. For nations there is a weighing time. National sins demand national punishments.[151]

Spurgeon again expressed his struggle with the "bloodshed, tyranny, and war" of the British Empire in his homeland and the slave-based system across the Atlantic in the American South but warned that "an hour of retribution draweth nigh."[152]

As this work goes into the warning of mixing Christianity with government, Christians must stand as a portion of the citizenry committed to praying for their governmental leaders. In this area, Christians must mix these two realms!

The Church Must Beware of Mixing Christianity with Political Movements

To align God's kingdom with the kingdoms of this world is to corrupt the Kingdom work taking place. In an 1863 sermon, Spurgeon preached on the trial of Jesus and showed from historical works that Rome's agenda and ambitions were tainted, unable to embrace the truth of Jesus' teaching and ministry due to their corruption:

> Now, that was a thing no Roman understood; for a hundred years before Pilate came, Jugurtha said of the city of Rome, "a city for sale;" bribery, corruption, falsehood, treachery, villany, these were the gods of Rome, and truth had fled the seven hills, the

---

[151] Spurgeon, "The Scales of Judgment," *NPSP* 5:257 (1859).

[152] Spurgeon, "The Scales of Judgment."

very meaning of the word was scarcely known. So Pilate turned on his heel, and said, "What is truth?" As much as to say, "I am the procurator of this part of the country; all I care for is money." "What's truth?" I do not think he asked the question, "What is truth?" as some preach from it, as if he seriously desired to know what it really was, for surely he would have paused for the divine reply and not have gone away from Christ the moment afterwards.[153]

Spurgeon's autobiography notes a publication from October 9, 1880, entitled the *Boy's Own Paper,* which published silhouettes of those considered the greatest celebrities of the age. Among the number were prime ministers William Gladstone and Benjamin Disraeli. Yet, in the center of the nine silhouettes was Mr. Spurgeon himself![154] Bebbington notes how Spurgeon was "the most popular preacher of the day," not surprising considering how religion played a large part in Victorian England.[155] Given his celebrity status, one could understand if he succumbed to the temptation of absorbing and reveling in the praises of men and dipping his toe into the political realm more than he did. Yet, he continually reminded his congregation of mixing, or worse surrendering, the mission of Christianity to that of an earthly government.

In a sermon at the Crystal Palace soon after the mutiny in India in 1857, Spurgeon lamented at how gospel mission work was impeded due to the presence of Great Britain in India. To the surprise of many in the audience, the twenty-four-year-old preacher made this comment regarding the nature of Britain:

Did you ever hear of a nation under British rule being converted to God? Mr. Moffat and our great friend Dr. Livingstone have been laboring in Africa with great success, and many have been converted. Did you ever hear of Kaffir tribes protected by England, ever being converted? It is only a people that have been

---

[153] Spurgeon, "The Greatest Trial on Record," *MTP* 9:495 (1863).

[154] Spurgeon, *Autobiography*, Vol. 4; quoted in Morden, "C.H. Spurgeon and Suffering," 306.

[155] Bebbington, *Evangelicalism in Modern Britain: A History from 1730s to the 1980s*, 145.

left to themselves, and preached to by men as men, that have been brought to God.[156]

Earlier in this sermon, alluded to in Chapter One, Spurgeon made these remarks as well,

I believe that British rule there, has been useful in many ways. I shall not deny the civilizing influence of European society; or that great things have been done for humanity; but I do assert, and can prove it, that there would have been greater probability of the Gospel spreading in India if it had been let alone, than there has been ever since the domination of Great Britain.[157]

Spurgeon never allowed to mistake his love for his country, prime minister, and the Crown for the Kingdom of God. Spurgeon possessed a keen awareness of the differences between the two and never fell into the trap of mixing the two, even as he was fully engaged in influencing political matters. "Do not give yourselves up to party spirit… To live for a political party is unworthy of a man who professes to be a Christian… What is the science of diplomacy but the art of deceit?"[158]

Even with this sentiment, Spurgeon respected and admired William E. Gladstone, the prime minister of his day, because of Gladstone's desire to please God in the realm of politics. Gladstone biographer Philip Magnus held that Gladstone's political career sought to bring the principles of Christianity into all parts of political life.[159] This made Spurgeon's connection with political life easier due to the shared beliefs (and, yes, friendship) between himself and Gladstone. Lewis Drummond noted that in the Victorian age, "Some clergymen and church members believed that politics were just too dirty a business in which to be involved. Spurgeon proved to be the antithesis of that attitude."[160] Spurgeon sought to promote a biblical

---

[156] Spurgeon, "The Independence of Christianity," *NPSP* 3:149.

[157] Spurgeon, "The Independence of Christianity."

[158] Spurgeon, "What God Cannot Do!", *MTP* 28:92 (1882).

[159] Magnus, *Gladstone, A Biography*, xi. Quoted in Drummond, *Spurgeon: Prince of Preachers*, 511.

[160] Drummond, *Spurgeon*, 514.

worldview in dealing with individual issues rather than someone beholden to a party for the party's sake, regardless of the issue.

The Anglican Church

Of all the issues with which Spurgeon, a Baptist Dissenter, objected, the most stringent was the system of the Anglican Church, whose head is the reigning monarch.[161] In 1534, the Act of Supremacy was an act of Parliament expedited by Henry VIII, a move expedited not due to his disagreement with Rome (for he himself argued strongly against the Reformation doctrines of Luther), but rather due to Henry's desire to annul Catherine of Aragon (his brother's widow) and marry Anne Boleyn—for Catherine could not provide Henry the necessary heir.[162] The Pope had refused the annulment due to Catherine being the aunt of Charles V of Spain (a dignitary the Pope dared not cross). When Cranmer, the Archbishop of Canterbury, took counsel with the prominent Catholic universities of the day, they believed Henry's marriage to Catherine was not legitimate.[163] Those bishops who opposed this legislation (and among them was chancellor Sir Thomas More) were beheaded. While at the time, surrendering the legislative decisions to the monarch and ultimately severing their relationship to Rome and the Pope's influence, the marriage of state and church stood as a troublesome one due to its scandalous and suspect beginnings.

Spurgeon delivered many sermons preaching against this pervasive presence in English life, calling this "first among the evils of the age ... the return of superstition [whose] mischief is in the Catechism and the service book [i.e., the *Book of Common Prayer*]."[164] He felt this system destroyed souls and created a tyranny against dissenting but faithful churches over the centuries.

---

[161] This work will address Spurgeon's unrest with the Anglican Church in Chapter Five on the topic of religious liberty.

[162] Gonzalez, *The Story of Christianity: The Early Church to the Present Day,* 72.

[163] Gonzalez, *The Story of Christianity,* 72.

[164] Spurgeon, *An All-Around Ministry: Addresses to Ministers and Students,* 71. Chapter Five will address in more detail Spurgeon's concern about the *Book of Common Prayer.*

Spurgeon editorialized on the separation of the Established Church and the Dissenters in his sermon on Jude 19 on December 13, 1859:

> We did not separate ourselves—we were turned out. Dissenters did not separate themselves from the Church of England, from the Episcopal church; but when the Act of Uniformity was passed, they were turned out of their pulpits. Our forefathers were as sound Churchmen as any in the world, but they could not take in all the errors of the Prayer Book, and they were therefore hounded to their graves by the intolerance of the conforming professors.[165]

Ecclesiastically, Spurgeon struggled with how the Anglican Church embraced the doctrine of baptismal regeneration. Gregory Wills observes that Spurgeon's local church polity consisted of three convictions: regenerate church membership, believer's baptism, and congregational church polity. While all three are important, Wills contended (and Spurgeon would contend as well) that one was primary. "[R]egeneration was the only essential element of local church polity. Congregational polity, and especially believer's baptism, promoted regenerate church membership"[166] In response to a Spurgeon talk that rebuked the Anglican Church for their adherence to infant baptism, he received many arguments embracing this religious rite. Spurgeon volleyed back:

> I marvel that a Church so learned as the Anglican, cannot produce something a little more worthy of the point in hand… The whole question is, do you believe that baptism regenerates? If so—prove that your belief is Scriptural! Do you believe that

---

[165] Spurgeon, "The Holy Spirit and the One Church," *NPSP* 4:167 (1857). The Act of Uniformity to which Spurgeon refers was passed by Parliament in 1662, calling for a strict adherence of churches to conform to the rites outlined in the Book of Common Prayer. This adherence was required for those who sought employment in the offices of government or churches. Approximately 2,000 clergymen refused to conform (thus the moniker "dissenter") and thus lost their churches.

[166] Wills, "The Ecclesiology of Charles H. Spurgeon," 67.

baptism does not regenerate? Then justify your swearing that it does. Who will reply to this? He shall merit and bear the palm.[167]

Spurgeon desired an ecclesiastical simplicity of building a church around Christ and His Word, a situation markedly absent in the state church. "He hated the shame and mere display; abhorred a State Church, and said so in many a sermon... He seemed to take special delight in shattering all ecclesiastical authority and many things held sacred by men; in fact, he was an iconoclast and delighted in idol breaking."[168]

In an 1877 sermon, Spurgeon spoke more expressly of his desire to stick to "the simple truth of his glorious gospel" over and against the pomp that comes with the worship found in the Anglican Church:

Human history brings before us an abundance of instances in which, nevertheless, though scribes, priests, bishops, pontiffs, and popes condemned the truth, it was just as sure, and became as triumphant, as it had a right to do. There stands the one lone man, and there are all the great ones around him—men of authority and reputation, sanctity and pomp—and they unanimously deny that he can ever sit at the right hand of God: "But, nevertheless," saith he, "hereafter ye shall see the Son of man at the right hand of power." He spoke the truth: His declaration has been most gloriously fulfilled hitherto. Even thus over the neck of clergy, priests, pontiffs, popes, his triumphant chariot of salvation shall still roll, and the truth—the simple truth of his glorious gospel—shall, despite them all, win the day, and reign over the sons of men.[169]

Spurgeon reminded his congregation that only One reigns who is worthy of such pomp and circumstance, Jesus Christ. For anyone to take this glory and put it on any Earthly man, even if that man represented an ecclesiastical authority intending to bring glory to

---

[167] Spurgeon, "Children Came to Christ, Not to the Font," *MTP* 10:581 (1864).

[168] Hall, "Spurgeon as I Knew Him," 139.

[169] Spurgeon, "Nevertheless. Hereafter," *MTP* 23:1364 (1877).

God, was blasphemous for Spurgeon. In the *Sword and the Trowel*, Spurgeon used his gift of picturesque metaphors: "I remember reading about a three-headed dog which kept the gates of hell, but I never dreamed of a two-headed church till I heard of the Anglican Establishment."[170] In his book on Spurgeon's pastoral theology, Tom Nettles reflected Spurgeon's attitude toward this problematic structure: "*No* head or governor can share authority with Jesus over his church, its truths, its prayers, its worship, or its members."[171]

Not Like the Proud
Monarchs of the Earth

Never once did anyone find Jesus intimidated or in awe of the authorities in place during His earthly life, not even one as powerful as the Roman Empire. Christ operated by another country whose laws and edicts took precedence over any other, even those of the formidable Roman Empire. Repeatedly, Jesus differentiated his rule from the presiding role of Caesar. The best example of Jesus' political mindset is found in Mark 10:42–45 after Jesus reprimanded James and John for their request to sit on both sides of Christ's throne when he comes in his glory:

> You know that those who are considered rulers of the Gentiles lord it over them, and their great ones exercise authority over them. But it shall not be so among you. But whoever would be great among you must be your servant, and whoever would be first among you must be slave of all. For even the Son of Man came not to be served but to serve, and to give his life as a ransom for many" (Mk 10:42–45).

Jesus reprimanded the disciples for absorbing the culture of the "rulers of the Gentiles" to such a degree that they assumed the culture of the Kingdom of God operated the same way. The disciples looked to the strategies of the earthly leaders and disregarded the strategy of Jesus, who called them out of this world. Jesus himself

---

[170] Spurgeon, SS, 8:74.
[171] Nettles, *Living by Revealed Faith*, 511.

did not conduct himself like other monarchs, showing by nature, calling, and example a demonstration of servant leadership. Spurgeon drove home this point,

> In the height of his grandeur he is not like the proud monarchs of earth. The patient ass he prefers to the noble charger; and he is more at home with the common people than with the great. In his grandest pageant, in his capital city, he was still consistent with his meek and lowly character, for he came "riding upon an ass." He rode through Jerusalem in state; but what lowliness marked the spectacle![172]

The principles of heaven and of earth operate differently from each other. As he called others to set their personal agendas aside, Jesus set his glory aside, not due to any intimidating force emanating from Rome, but to do the will of his Father in heaven in rescuing his people from their sins (Mt 1:21).

Reflecting Upon
American "Evangelicalism"

This work has so far reflected on Spurgeon's view of heavenly citizenship, earthly citizenship, and how the two citizenships work together. The next question this chapter must answer is, how do Spurgeon's conclusions answer the challenges today's American evangelical churches face in understanding their roles in heavenly and earthly citizenship? This section will discuss the parallel situations surrounding Spurgeon in nineteenth-century Victorian England and the situations surrounding American evangelical Christians in the twenty-first century.

Appropriating Christian
Language to Political Life

In Spurgeon's time (and since 1532), one would not be surprised at the use of Christian language in political life, given the proximity

---

[172] Spurgeon, "Our Lowly King," *MTP* 31 (1885).

between church and government. When examining the American political landscape, this present generation may be surprised at the prevalence of biblical language appropriated in political speeches.

In evaluating the motive of the Founding Fathers' aim for religion's role in the United States, Jon Meacham encapsulates their rationale well: "Given the world in which they lived—a time of divisive arguments about God and politics—the Founders paid close attention, for their time is like our time, and they found a way to honor religion's place in the life of the nation while giving people the freedom to believe as they wish, and not merely tolerate someone else's faith, but to respect it."[173] Thus, the original defining document of our country, the Declaration of Independence, invokes language such as being "endowed by our Creator with certain inalienable rights," "nature's God," and "all men are created equal." The religious language did not expressly equate to *Christian* language but was general enough to include all strains of religious belief. As Alexis de Tocqueville observed after his tour of America in 1833, "I do not know if all Americans have faith in their religion—for who can read to the bottom of hearts?—but I am sure that they believe it necessary to the maintenance of republican institutions. This opinion does not belong only to one class of citizens or to one party, but to the entire nation; one finds it in all ranks." [174] Even in the nineteenth-century, religious morality informed governmental agenda and vice versa.

One of the key tenets of the United States was the belief originated by Thomas Jefferson (1734–1826) of separation of church and state, a principle with which (one could argue) Spurgeon would agree. Though Jefferson penned this principle soon after becoming president in response to a religious liberty concern from the Danbury (CT) Baptist Association in 1802, his response sought to set their mind at ease by saying, "Adhering to this expression of the supreme will of the nation on behalf of the rights of conscience, I shall see with sincere satisfaction the progress of those sentiments

---

[173] Meacham, *American Gospel: God, the Founding Fathers, and the Making of a Nation,* 6.

[174] de Tocqueville, *Democracy in America,* ed. and trans. Mansfield and Winthrop, 280. Quoted in Noll, *America's God: From Jonathan Edwards to Abraham Lincoln,* 10.

which tend to restore to man all his natural rights, convinced he has no natural right in opposition to his social duties." Jefferson reassured the people that the legislative branch dealt with "actions, and not opinions."[175] The concept of separation of church and state, though not found in the U.S. Constitution, would play a pivotal interpretive role over the last century in cases that have appeared before the U.S. Supreme Court. The curious appropriation of religious language in political campaigns and speeches has often brought calls that have violated this treasured (though un-Constitutional) tenet.

While not expressly informed by Scripture, a residue of biblical morality informs the American evangelical church's particular ethic when evaluating and ultimately voting for a particular candidate—something that Spurgeon encouraged, for this informed his decision to support William Gladstone for Prime Minister. However, to mesh a pseudo-biblical morality with a sense of nationalistic/patriotic pride develops a type of cultural Christianity that is more American than Christian. Stephen Prothero contributes much to how religions, specifically Christianity in America, have become as much American as Christian. In his insightful book *American Jesus: How the Son of God Became a National Icon*, Prothero observes how, in America, Jesus has been melded into the story of American history. "To hold Jesus up to the mirror of American culture is to conduct a Rorschach test of ever-changing national sensibilities. What Americans have seen in him has been an expression of their own hopes and fears—a reflection not simply of some 'wholly other' divinity but also of themselves and their nation."[176] This statement is rather telling—Jesus is an expression of American hopes and fears, rather than our hopes and fears surrendering to the lordship of Jesus. The temptation for all is to allow our earthly citizenship to influence and shade the view of our heavenly citizenship without ever realizing the transformation.

The American evangelical church must beware of the cultural partnerships it makes, for some candidates could use

---

[175] Jefferson, "Jefferson's Letter to the Danbury Baptists," *Information Bulletin*, June 1998, 57:6.

[176] Prothero, *American Jesus: How the Son of God Became a National Icon*, 2003.

religious language not out of any personal piety but simply to procure their vote. In 1961, John F. Kennedy, an avowed Roman Catholic, surrounded his candidacy for President with much conversation and concern about how much his religion would influence policy. In reflecting on Kennedy's inauguration speech in 1961, Robert Bellah insightfully observes how Kennedy continued to use religious language, but to what end?

> He did not refer to any religion in particular. He did not refer to Jesus Christ, or to Moses, or to the Christian church; certainly he did not refer to the Catholic church. In fact, his only reference was to the concept of God, a word that almost all Americans can accept but that means so many different things to so many different people that it is almost an empty sign. Is this not just another indication that in America religion is considered vaguely to be a good thing, but that people care so little about it that it has lost any content whatever? Isn't Dwight Eisenhower reported to have said "Our government makes no sense unless it is founded in a deeply felt religious faith-and I don't care what it is," and isn't that a complete negation of any real religion?[177]

Spurgeon would note that the only true religion is that of the Christian religion, with Jesus reigning as king. Those governmental and ecclesiastical alliances of the Anglican Church were the reality of Spurgeon's time (as opposed to the "wall" between church and state in America). The attempt by politicians, beginning with our Founding Fathers, to use this language to bring God and country together can work only if, according to Spurgeon, that "God" was the God of the Bible who pointed clearly to Jesus Christ.

Thus, regarding the language used in the Declaration of Independence forward, some Christian zealots did not believe this language went far enough as did those with worldviews that leaned secular. Politicians both then and now were certainly aware of the ebb and flow of the culture in which they operated and just as certainly sought to procure their votes. Yet, the Founding Fathers

---

[177] Bellah, "Religion in America," Daedalus, *Journal of the American Academy of Arts and Sciences,* Winter 1967, 96-1, 1. The quote of Dwight Eisenhower is found in Will Herberg, *Protestant-Catholic-Jew*, 97.

sought to make the United States a place where all could worship in the faith of their conscience. Soon after and even today, each worldview vies for prominence and priority. Yet the follower of Christ should not equate the religious language found in our documents and in addresses from politicians as an ascent to Christianity.

Fellow Christians are Closer in
Relation than Biological Siblings

Political and geographical boundaries exist for God's sovereign purposes. However, they do not exist when dealing with followers of Christ, for Scripture shows that all followers of Christ are brothers and sisters in Christ, regardless of earthly citizenship, background, or race. Patriotic zeal meshed with one's Christian walk continues the problematic trajectory of combining the spiritual and earthly allegiances as either equals (see the "God and Country" motif many hold) or, more tragically, seeing their earthly citizenship as more valuable than their heavenly citizenship. One may remember the clip in the movie *Chariots of Fire* when Eric Liddell refused to run his race on Sunday in the 1924 Olympics, noting, "God made countries, God makes kings, and rules by which they govern. And those rules say that the Sabbath is His. And I for one intend to keep it that way." One of the English dignitaries, Lord Cadogan, replied, "In my day it was King first and God after."[178]

The church of Jesus Christ, as Spurgeon has clearly articulated and this Romanian pastor reaffirmed, transcends any institution the state offers. The church is not a state institution, again to which Spurgeon struggled with the Anglican Church found in his own country, but an embassy of heaven here on earth, as Michael Horton noted:

The central message of Christianity is not a worldview, a way of life, or a program for personal and societal change; it is a gospel....That is why the New Testament refers to the offices of apostle (official representative), preacher, and evangelist,

---

[178] Bauer, *Chariots of Fire,* Warner Bros., 1981.

describing ministers as heralds, ambassadors, and witnesses. Their job is to get the story right and then report it, ensuring that the message is delivered by word (preaching) and deed (sacrament). And the result is a church, an embassy of the Triune God in the midst of this passing evil age, with the whole people of God giving witness to God's mighty acts of redemption.[179]

Yet, another potent is that of family, most particularly identified in the doctrine of adoption. Yes, even those who are not biologically connected or even socio-politically connected find themselves connected more closely due to the redemptive and adoptive work of Christ. Spurgeon made the doctrine of adoption abundantly clear, a clarity most needed to understand how one must construct a Christ-centered ethic toward the vulnerable:

> Adoption is that act of God, whereby men who were by nature the children of wrath, even as others, and were of the lost and ruined family of Adam, are from no reason in themselves, but entirely of the pure grace of God, translated out of the evil and black family of Satan, and brought actually and virtually into the family of God; so that they take his name, share the privileges of sons, and they are to all intents and purposes the actual offspring and children of God.[180]

The establishment of the biblical view of spiritual adoption as sons of God is critical to understanding God's system of redemption in regard to building his spiritual kingdom filled with heavenly citizens. Spurgeon's work reflects Galatians 3:28–29: "There is neither Jew nor Greek, there is neither slave nor free, there is no male nor female, for you are all one in Christ Jesus. And if you are Christ's, then you are Abraham's offspring, heirs according to promise." This kingdom seeks to rescue image-bearers of God, regardless of their racial or social background.

Consider the monarchical hereditary system in place in England, a system ingrained in all British citizens since birth. In this

---

[179] Horton, *Christless Christianity: The Alternative Gospel of the American Church*, 105.

[180] Spurgeon, "Adoption," *MTP* 7:360 (1859).

system, only one at any given time is rightly considered the heir to the throne. Spurgeon sought to help his congregation (and readers of his sermons) understand the nature of God's adoption as heirs:

> There is but one that can claim the heir's rights, and the heir's title. It is not so in the family of God. Man as a necessary piece of political policy, may give to the heir that which surely he can have not more real right to in the sight of God, than the rest of the family—may give him all the inheritance, while his brethren, equally true born, may go without; but it is not so in the family of God. All God's children are heirs, however numerous the family, and he that shall be born of God last, shall be as much his heir as he who was born first.[181]

Remember, too, Spurgeon's conviction regarding England's status as greater than "Israel of old?" This mindset was also ingrained into the minds and hearts of lifelong British citizens. Yet, Spurgeon showed God's system of those who were heirs, not relegated to only one person but heirs from every walk and status of life:

> The Lord has been pleased to separate many of us to himself and bring us into his visible church, so that we dwell within that "garden walled around, chosen and made peculiar ground." Herein is no small deed of love. Aliens are made fellow citizens with the saints and of the household of God. Yet, much more than this has been done for true believers in the blood of Jesus.[182]

"Aliens are made fellow citizens with the saints and of the household of God"—what a statement! Britain would never consider this notion when discussing inheriting the throne, but look at what Jesus accomplished on the behalf of all who would trust in His work.

Spurgeon sought not only to instill God's economy into the hearts and minds of his listeners and readers, but he also coupled this privilege with their responsibility as new citizens of heaven. In an 1858 sermon, Spurgeon preached on the Macedonian call found

---

[181] Spurgeon, "The Sons of God," *NPSP* 6:339 (1860).
[182] Spurgeon, "Nearness to God," *MTP* 15:851 (1869).

in Acts 16:6–10, where the vision came to the apostle Paul for the missionaries to "Come over to Macedonia and help us." Spurgeon took the opportunity to stand as "the heathen's spokesman, and very earnestly ask you to come and help him."

> Methinks, I will stand here as a heathen this morning, and I say to you as if I had not heard the gospel. "Ye Christians of Britain! ye highly favored ones, who know the name of Jesus and prove the power of the Spirit, preach the gospel to us, for we are men like yourselves. What though our skin be of a color less fair than your own? Yet he fashioneth our hearts alike. Oh tell us not, because we feed on the locust, and eat the serpent, that therefore we are not of your kith and kin! 'Not that which goeth into a man defileth a man.' It is true, our kings and princes are only fit to rank with your beggars; but oh! God hath made of one blood all nations that dwell upon the face of the earth.[183]

Merely receiving Christ's redemptive work without seeing the subsequent responsibility in sharing this with others was unthinkable to Spurgeon. He expertly takes the theatrical mantle of playing the role of a "heathen" to make a needed point that American evangelical churches would due heed—that the providence of God that brought the gospel to England now turns into a responsibility to take the gospel to other nations, regardless of background, cultural practices, or race. By God's sovereign will, he sent missionaries to bring the gospel to the land that would become Great Britain, filled with tyranny and bloodshed, to fulfill his own purposes. Part of those purposes lie in taking the gospel that was brought to them elsewhere in fulfillment of the Great Commission! When it comes to the Great Commission, Christianity has no borders.

---

[183] Spurgeon, "The Cry of the Heathen," *NPSP* 4:189 (1858).

A Borderless Christianity
Fueled by the Great Commission

Neither imperialism nor any form of nationalism supersedes Christ's call to go as Spirit-empowered witnesses to "Jerusalem, and in all of Judea, and Samaria, and to the ends of the earth" (Acts 1:8). While one does not see the reaction on the faces of the disciples when Christ gave this command, one does read previously in Acts 1:3 that "He presented himself alive to them after his suffering by many proofs, appearing to them during forty days and speaking about the kingdom of God." Each disciple was (to a greater or lesser degree) devoted to Israel; thus the asking of the question in Acts 1:6, "Lord, will you at this time restore the kingdom of Israel?" All through the Gospels, the disciples were continually confused as to the nature of Christ's kingdom rule, believing this rule would overthrow the present rule of Rome. Even after forty days of learning about the kingdom of God, these prejudices and passions were not easily shaken. Rather than provide information as to the timing of when this Kingdom would inevitably take place, Christ told his disciples that they would be used to spread the Kingdom to other sociopolitical bases and cultures. Rather than all the nations coming to the church, "the Israel of God" (Galatians 6:16) would go to the nations in fulfillment of the Abrahamic covenant in Genesis 12:1–3 and the Mosaic covenant (Exodus 19–24), named after Moses, God's chosen leader to rescue the Israelites from the tyranny of Egypt to freedom in the Promised Land:

> No more have we the law upon stone, but the Spirit writes the precept upon the fleshy tablets of the heart. Moses on the mount can only tell us what to do, but Jesus ascended on high pours out the power to do it. Now we are not under the law, but under grace, and the Spirit is our guiding force. In the church of God our rule is not according to the letter of a law, but according to the Spirit of the Lord.[184]

---

[184] Spurgeon, "Pentecost," *MTP* 30 (1884).

Spurgeon's life and ministry made certain aspects of Christianity abundantly clear. Social reform in and even *of* the culture is the primary mission of the church, and while there is the temptation of using governmental or non-profit works at the exclusion of preaching the gospel, Spurgeon rightly believed that social reform occurred as an outgrowth of the gospel. In the American evangelical church, another line of thinking in regard to ministry exists: the gospel is merely for the eternal and spiritual aspects of a person, not for the earthly and temporal. This entails a focus on preparing others for the hereafter while disregarding the here and now.

Thomas Kidd in his most helpful work, *What is an Evangelical?,* describes this much-debated term as, "Evangelicals are born-again Protestants who cherish the Bible as the Word of God and who emphasize a personal relationship with Jesus Christ through the Holy Spirit." Kidd rightly gives a definition as a springboard to a movement that takes on a multitude of directions. While this word "evangelical" comes from the word that means "gospel" or "good news," as in a herald in the town square who pronounced a victory of the army that won a battle on the people's behalf, the word came into common usage as a result of a *political* campaign. An article from *The Atlantic,* Jonathan Merritt notes that the word "evangelical pops up in American media to describe everything from mega-churches to voting blocs." [185] During the Great Awakening of the 1730s and 1740s, evangelicalism came to symbolize a desire to convert unbelievers to the faith.

While it is beyond the scope of this work to trace the history of evangelicalism Kidd, in his work mentioned previously, tracks the reform movement to modern times. Kidd pointed out that in 1976, the Gallup Organization began asking people if they had been "born again," marking not only the "emergence of *evangelical* as a common term in news coverage of politics [yet] was [also] a major landmark in the development of the contemporary evangelical crisis." [186] A crisis indeed! In the modern era of the United States, common usage began from a *political* campaign, not a religious one!

---

[185] Jonathan Merritt, "Defining 'Evangelical,'" *The Atlantic.*
[186] Kidd, *What is an Evangelical? The History of a Movement in Crisis,* Kindle Location 1628.

This stands as a landmark distinction as the momentum of the evangelical political movement in ushering Ronald Reagan into the presidency in 1980 and a number of "culture war controversies: school prayer, the [Equal Rights Amendment], homosexual rights, gambling, pornography, abortion, and other concerns" [187] — embraced mostly by white evangelicals. Among black evangelicals, the issues would overlap slightly, but the issues of racism and white evangelicals embracing of slavery, Jim Crow laws, and segregation (as prominent white evangelicals such as Jerry Falwell, Sr., and Bob Jones, Sr., accepted as valuable to society) separated them from their white evangelical brothers and sisters. Tom Skinner began preaching on social justice as an outgrowth of the gospel, but white evangelicals deemed him too political as he began to address their social injustices.

At the culmination of all things, Christ will establish his universal kingdom including every nation on earth. While one's earthly citizenships entail specific responsibilities as mortal citizens, the heavenly citizenship of Christ's disciples obliges them to traverse any and every border for earthly citizens to meet and surrender to the King of the Universe. Christ told his disciples, "All authority in heaven and earth has been given to me" (Mt 28:18). In an 1861 sermon, Spurgeon's missionary zeal came full force to his listeners as he reminded them of Christ's commission:

Oh! I would that the Church could hear the Saviour addressing these words to her now; for the words of Christ are living words, not having power in them yesterday alone, but to-day also. The injunctions of the Saviour are perpetual in their obligation; they were not binding upon apostles merely, but upon us also, and upon every Christian does this yoke fall, "Go ye, therefore, and teach all nations, baptizing them in the name of the Father, and of the Son, and of the Holy Ghost." We are not exempt to-day from the service of the first followers of the Lamb; our marching orders are the same as theirs, and our Captain requires from us obedience as prompt and perfect as from them. Oh that his

---

[187] Kidd, *What is an Evangelical?* Kindle Location 1642.

message may not fall upon deaf ears, or be heard by stolid souls![188]

Whenever the earthly citizenship trumps the heavenly citizenship, then the priorities and even the prejudices of the former affect the Christian's perceived obligations of the latter. "Gentile and Jew, African and European—they shall all meet at the cross, the common centre of our entire manhood; for Christ is lifted up, and he is drawing all men unto him."[189] Since this is the case, all believers everywhere recognize the transcendent duty and delight of submitting to his authority and serving fellow imagebearers of God who will prayerfully become children of the Heavenly Father.

Spurgeon preached one Sunday on Deuteronomy 32:21, which reads,

> They have made me jealous with what is no god;
> They have provoked me to anger with their idols.
> So I will make them jealous with those who are no people;
> I will provoke them to anger with a foolish nation (ESV).

As the people of Israel were ready to enter the Promised Land after a contentious relationship with the One who delivered them, God foretold the trajectory of their lives which would be marked by persistent disobedience. Spurgeon reminded his congregation again (as alluded to previously in this work) that God gave the gospel to the nation for that nation to take the gospel to other nations—and also reminded them of how, at the time, all nations (though outside the covenant of Abraham) would jealously be brought in:

> Truly this is fulfilled in these days when the gospel line hath gone out throughout all the earth, and its words unto the ends of the earth; and this our own foolish nation, this once barbarous people which seemed shut out from God, worshipping idols with all the cruel rites of the Druids, has been brought into covenant with God and made to rejoice in him. Degraded heathen in all

---

[188] Spurgeon, "The Missionaries' Charge and Charta," *MTP* 7: 383 (1861).

[189] Spurgeon, "The Marvellous Magnet," *MTP* 29:1717 (1880).

lands have become believers, and so shall all nations be brought believingly to Jesus' feet, that Israel may be angered and provoked to jealousy until her time shall come, when she shall look on him whom she hath pierced, and shall mourn for him, and turn to him with full purpose of heart.[190]

The gospel goes into all nations, regardless of their station in life, and have given testimony to the redemptive work of Christ.

Conclusion

Spurgeon helps provide the modern American evangelical church a biblical clarity of dual citizenship which, in turn, feeds a channel in the construction of a gospel-centered ethic toward the vulnerable. The next channel under consideration is the topic of racism. Sadly, the world's history has been marked by certain groups believing that they are superior to others due to their race. Part of Spurgeon's trouble with imperialistic England lay in this belief as they conquered countries all over the globe based on this supposed superiority. In the next chapter, Spurgeon will provide biblical clarity regarding God's view of how different races interact.

---

[190] Spurgeon, "Christ's Universal Kingdom, and how it cometh," *MTP* 26 (1880).

Spurgeon's Ethic on Racism

The Christian church has dealt with the issue and implications of racism ever since its inception. For American evangelicals in the nineteenth century, Spurgeon would provide fuel for the abolitionists and fodder for the American Southern slaveholders—not to mention fueling animosity of the churches in the American South that practiced the institution of slavery. For American evangelicals in the late twentieth- and early twenty-first-centuries navigating the waters of racism that still exists in churches and in their culture, they can look to Charles Spurgeon, who gave a template for a gospel-centered ethic toward the racial strife with which many struggle today.

Spurgeon lived in an era of two minds. The first was that which he inherited—an England that was freed from the injustices of slavery a year before he was born, thanks to the work of William Wilberforce (1759–1833). The second was a mind whose worldview was consistent with the philosophy of an Empire whose goal was that "the sun would never set on the British Empire."[191] As noted in the previous chapter on nationalism, the belief in the superiority of England over and against other nations and races stoked the insidious fires of religious, cultural, and even racial supremacy. Though slavery was now illegal, most of Britain's colonial expansion had been built on the backs of slavery and indentured servitude for centuries. Yet, for those who held to Christianity and for many in the political realm, Wilberforce's passion and worldview still captured their hearts and minds. This work will address the influence of Wilberforce and another influence that

---

[191] Macartney, *An Account of Ireland in 1773. By a Late Chief Secretary of that Kingdom*, 55; quoted Kenny, *ed. Ireland and the British Empire*, 72.

would, sadly, capture the imagination of another sector of England: Academia.

The concept of natural selection, a.k.a. Darwinism, named after the natural scientist Charles Darwin (1809–1882), arrived on the British scene. Darwin's theory of macroevolution and the progression of species into higher forms fueled racism and Anglo supremacy in academics and politics. Whereas Wilberforce died in 1833, Darwin's trip to the Galapagos Islands in 1835 influenced generations after. Spurgeon had much to say about both "minds," both the positives and the dangers of embracing one or the other.

The previous chapter addressed a gospel-centered ethic toward the vulnerable regarding nationalism. This chapter moves toward an offspring of nationalism; that is, racism. Nationalism believes in the superiority of a nation or a people group, which may easily translate into racism, which is a belief in the superiority of one race over another. When Spurgeon came to Christ during that blizzard in January 1850, the supply preacher of the morning preached from Isaiah 45:22: "Look unto me, and be ye saved, all the ends of the earth." While Spurgeon certainly focused on the first portion of this verse, over time his ministry would demonstrate a conviction to send messengers of salvation to "all the ends of the earth," regardless of race or nationality.

The Positive Influence
of William Wilberforce

All of Christian England and all political abolitionists regardless of their faith saw Wilberforce as a hero, a Christian who led with his conscience not from the pulpit but from his work in politics, which spanned forty-five years (1780–1825), twenty-eight of those years as a Member of Parliament (MP) from Yorkshire. In 1785, one year after becoming an MP, Wilberforce became an evangelical Christian—a change that would inform his political agendas for the rest of his life. From then on, Wilberforce noted, "It is of God's unmerited goodness that I am selected as the agent of usefulness."[192]

---

[192] R.I. and S. Wilberforce, *The Life of William Wilberforce* Vol 5., 129. Quoted in McMullen, "William Wilberforce: 'Agent of Usefulness,'" 40.

His speech in 1789 expertly laid out the rationale for the abolition of slavery in England—a speech that still resonates in the hearts and minds of all who would take up the banner of social justice and freedom with a single-minded focus:

> But when I reflect, however, on the encouragement which I have had, through the whole course of a long and laborious examination of this question, and how much candour I have experienced, and how conviction has increased within my own mind, in proportion as I have advanced in my labours;—when I reflect, especially, that however averse any gentleman may now be, yet we shall all be of one opinion in the end;—when I turn myself to these thoughts, I take courage—I determine to forget all my other fears, and I march forward with a firmer step in the full assurance that my cause will bear me out, and that I shall be able to justify upon the clearest principles, every resolution in my hand, the avowed end of which is, the total abolition of the slave trade.[193]

Whereas Darwin and his view of natural selection meant that humanity could advance and evolve without the help of a Creator, Wilberforce reflected on how humanity would devolve spiritually without the help of a Creator and Savior, thereby affecting a person's attitudes and behaviors in the culture in which they live:

> How on any principles of common reasoning, can we account for it, but by conceiving that man, since he came out of the hands of his Creator, has contracted a taint, and that the venom of this subtle poison has been communicated throughout the race of Adam, every where [sic] exhibiting incontestable marks of its fatal malignity [a desire to harm others]? Hence it has arisen, that the appetites deriving new strength, and the powers of reason and conscience being weakened, the latter have feebly

---

[193] Cobbett, "Debate on Mr. Wilberforce's Resolutions respecting the Slave Trade," *The Parliamentary History of England: from the Norman Conquest in 1066 to the year 1803*, 28.

and impotently pleaded against those forbidden indulgences which the former have solicited.[194]

For Spurgeon, William Wilberforce was a model Christian, which made him a model politician in his efforts toward reform:

And, I think, when Wilberforce went to the House of Commons, however he might ride, the bit of his horse was Holiness to the Lord. Since we cannot dispense with the ceremonial honor which surrounds governors, we must consecrate it, as long as kingdoms remain, it must be the prayer of Christians that the state may be a holy state, and that its officers and governors may be devout and upright men.[195]

In what William Wilberforce called his "manifesto," he penned a book in 1823 entitled, *An Appeal to the Religion, Justice, and Humanity of the Inhabitants of the British Empire, in Behalf of the Negro Slaves in the West Indies*. Writing with a telling combination of Christian charity and courage, he made his appeal:

I call upon them, as they shall hereafter answer, in the great day of account, for the use they shall have made of any power or influence with which Providence may have entrusted them, to employ their best endeavors, by all lawful and constitutional means, to mitigate, and, as soon as it may be safely done, to terminate the Negro Slavery of the British Colonies; a system of the grossest injustice, of the most heathenish irreligion and immorality, of the most unprecedented degradation, and unrelenting cruelty.[196]

---

[194] Wilberforce, *A practical view of the prevailing religious system of professed Christians: in the higher and middle classes in this country, contrasted with real Christianity*, 26.

[195] Spurgeon, "A Peal of Bells," *MTP* 7:399 (1861).

[196] William Wilberforce, *An Appeal to the Religion, Justice, and Humanity of the Inhabitants of the British Empire, in Behalf of the Negro Slaves in the West Indies* (London: J. Hatchard and Son, 1823), Kindle location 17.

Wilberforce poured out in this work his disgust at this vile institution, all the while appealing to the heart of the slaveowners in showing them the true nature of their profession "to produce impressions, not merely of contempt, but even of disgust and aversion."[197]

Wilberforce's life and political career influenced people on both sides of the Atlantic. Even in 1861 (twenty-eight years after Wilberforce's death), Spurgeon recognized: (1) Wilberforce was a strong follower of Christ by whom all direction concerning his policies flowed, and (2) the churches were praying for Wilberforce and set a template for believers for what should influence the politicians of the day—an influence that extended beyond the shores of England. For example, in his monthly magazine the *Douglass Monthly*, former slave and abolitionist Frederick Douglass invoked the name of Wilberforce in his article on what Americans should do if President Lincoln emancipated the slaves—the aim of the abolitionists and the bane of Southern plantation slaveholders:

> When you, our white fellow-countrymen, have attempted to do anything for us, it has generally been to deprive us of some right, power or privilege which you yourself would die before you would submit to have taken from you. When the planters of the West Indies used to attempt to puzzle the pure-minded Wilberforce with the question, How shall we get rid of slavery? his simple answer was, "quit stealing." In like manner, we answer those who are perpetually puzzling their brains with questions as to what shall be done with the Negro, "let him alone and mind your own business." If you see him plowing in the open field, leveling the forest, at work with the spade, a rake, a hoe, a pick-axe, or a bill—let him alone; he has a right to work.[198]

Later in a lecture, Douglass named "at least twenty-three British abolitionists and paid warm tributes especially to William

---

[197] Wilberforce, *An Appeal to the Religion,* Kindle location 121.

[198] Douglass, "What Shall Be Done if the Slaves are Emancipated?" *Douglass' Monthly,* January 1862.

Wilberforce and Thomas Clarkson."[199] Douglass, like Spurgeon, recognized Wilberforce's focus on eliminating this "stealing." Wilberforce, like with Spurgeon, motivated Douglass with a focus and sharpness of tone in speech and pen to abolish the egregious institution of slavery. Spurgeon recognized the role the church played in taking biblical truths from God's Word and applying them to all aspects of personal life and public culture. In an 1883 sermon, a half-century after Wilberforce's death, Spurgeon again invoked Wilberforce, showing that his influence still held sway over the hearts of his congregation and all who now followed Spurgeon. This work quoted the following quote in Chapter One and it bears repeating now:

A healthy church kills error, and tears in pieces evil. Not so very long ago our nation tolerated slavery in our colonies. Philanthropists endeavoured to destroy slavery; but when was it utterly abolished? It was when Wilberforce roused the church of God, and when the church of God addressed herself to the conflict, then she tore the evil thing to pieces. I have been amused with what Wilberforce said the day after they passed the Act of Emancipation. He merrily said to a friend when it was all done, "Is there not something else we can abolish?" That was said playfully, but it shows the spirit of the church of God. She lives in conflict and victory; her mission is to destroy everything that is bad in the land.[200]

Spurgeon showed his conviction that the church does indeed play a role in societal issues. He believed in the veracity and power of Scripture to change hearts, which, in turn, leads these transformed people to transform policy. As Spurgeon just noted, he understood how Wilberforce so "roused the church of God"[201] to end this evil practice that he was ready to tackle another issue, ready to "destroy everything that is bad in the land."[202] Sadly, many see the church as a haven from the world rather than a place to learn how to engage

---

[199] Blight, *Frederick Douglass: Prophet of Freedom*, 182.
[200] Spurgeon, "The Best War-Cry," *MTP* 29:1709 (1883).
[201] Spurgeon, "The Best War-Cry."
[202] Spurgeon, "The Best War-Cry."

the world's systems for the cause of Christ and the benefit of all the citizenry. In a sermon that described the church of Laodicea, Spurgeon admonished the church in a sermon from Revelation 3:17–18. "The Kingdom cannot come nor the Lord's banner be lifted high if the soldiers of his own army prove false and turn back in the day of battle. The time is come when judgment must begin at the house of God"[203]—echoing the apostle Peter's exhortation from his first epistle (1 Pt 4:17).

Spurgeon took seriously God's expectations for his church in English culture. "The Lord will be sanctified in them that come near to him, and if any enter the house to misbehave themselves, they will find that judgment begins at the house of God," again invoking 1 Peter 4:17.[204] From this same sermon, Spurgeon held to the notion that "below ... is the holy church militant, above it is the holy church triumphant."[205] Wilberforce influenced Spurgeon in his preaching and activism. Sadly, another influence arose, one which stood in contrast to the Scriptures.

The Troublesome Influence of Charles Darwin

Soon after Spurgeon's ministry began in London, a challenge arose about the origin and structure of humanity that would affect churches and schools until the present day. This challenge would rival the militancy of Wilberforce and Spurgeon. Naturalist Charles Darwin (1809–1882) published *On the Origin of Species* in 1859[206], which deviated from the origin narrative found in Scripture, describing the origin of all living things without the means of a Creator. Appealing to professional scientists who sought an origin narrative that did not include religious connections, Darwin's macroevolutionary theory of natural selection would in time become

---

[203] Spurgeon, "A Great Mistake and the Way to Rectify It," *MTP* 28:1677 (1882).

[204] Spurgeon, "Holiness, the Law of God's House," *MTP* 27:1618 (1881).

[205] Spurgeon, "Holiness."

[206] Darwin, *On The Origin of Species by Means of Natural Selection, or Preservation of Favoured Races in the Struggle for Life*.

accepted in all areas of science, literature, and politics. Spurgeon saw the dangerous effects this theory would have on the hearts of believers if left unchecked:

> The spiritual life cannot come to us by development from our old nature. I have heard a great deal about evolution and development, but I am afraid that if any one of us were to be developed to our utmost, apart from the grace of God, we should come out worse than before the development began. Our flesh would be apt to produce by evolution something exceedingly brutish and devilish.[207]

Darwin admitted when he penned *Origin of Species* that he did not have a significant amount of references on which to base his claims (possibly due to the pressure of publishing before a competitor who had arrived at similar conclusions), but in essence asked the readers to trust his conclusions, even with the errors that would make their way into the work.[208] While the scope of this work does not seek to evaluate all of Darwin's theories, one must interact with his overall influence in Great Britain and beyond regarding race:

> In considering the *Origin of Species*, it is quite conceivable that a naturalist, reflecting on the mutual affinities of organic beings, their embryological relations, their geographical distribution, geological succession, and other such facts, might conclude that each species had not been independently created, but had descended, like varieties, from other species. Nevertheless, such a conclusion, even if well-founded, would be unsatisfactory, until it could be shown how the innumerable species inhabiting this world have been modified, to acquire that perfection of

---

[207] Spurgeon, "The Singular Origin of a Christian Man," *MTP* 31:1829 (1885).

[208] Darwin, *Origin of Species*, 1. "This Abstract, which I now publish, must necessarily be imperfect. I cannot here give references and authorities for my several statements; and I must trust to the reader reposing some confidence in my accuracy. No doubt errors will have crept in, though I hope I have always been cautious in trusting to good authorities alone. I can here give only the general conclusions at which I have arrived with a few facts in illustration, but which, I hope, in most cases will suffice."

structure and coadaptation that most justly excites our admiration.[209]

In this small paragraph at the beginning of Darwin's work, one notes the differences between Darwin's theory and the Creation narrative of Genesis 1. Darwin conjectures that all species (humanity included) "descended ... from other species," while Genesis 1 conveys that all were created "according to their kinds" (Gn 1:21, 24, 25a, 25b, 25c), and then the creation of man "after our image, after our likeness" (1:26–28). The biblical worldview preaches that humanity is distinct from the other species and stands in the "image" and "likeness" of the Triune God.

While Darwin's view of the species' origins differed from that of Scripture, his view of humanity took a much sharper turn when discussing the different races. In 1871, Darwin published *The Descent of Man*. Given his understanding of the development of species from lower forms, Darwin arrived at the next logical step of his theory with his thoughts on the development of *homo sapiens*:

The Western nations of Europe ... now so immeasurably surpass their former savage progenitors [that they] stand at the summit of civilization... At some future period, not very distant as measured by centuries, the civilized races of man will almost certainly exterminate and replace throughout the world the savage races. At the same time the anthropomorphous apes, as Professor [Hermann] Schaaffhausen has remarked, will no doubt be exterminated. The break will then be rendered wider, for it will intervene between man in a more civilized state as we may hope, than the Caucasian and some ape as low as a baboon, instead of as at present between the negro or Australian and the gorilla.[210]

---

[209] Darwin, *Origin*, 1.

[210] Darwin, *The Descent of Man*, 105. Hermann Schaaffhausen is considered the founder of the discipline of paleoanthropology in Germany. In providing an explanation to Darwin's comments regarding "anthropomorphous apes," according to an abstract in *Anthropologgischer Anzeiger; Bericht uber die biologisch-anthropologische Literatur* 50:4, 1992, Schaaffhausen provided the "correct explanation of the Neanderthal man as a fossil human being."

Darwin's worldview of the races stood at the far end of the spectrum from what the Scriptures taught. Rather than seeing humans (regardless of race or geographical location) as image bearers of God, as Spurgeon preached, Darwin held that even among human beings a superiority/inferiority existed. So, while many in the church revered and sought to model their lives after Wilberforce, the scientific and political community allied themselves with Darwin and began to take the country in a different direction.

What became frustrating to Spurgeon, and other evangelical preachers who held to the narrative of Scripture, was that Darwin's philosophy began to infiltrate the churches. By the late 1880s, the last full decade of Spurgeon's ministry, he began to refer more and more to these teachings because more and more accepted them in the churches. In Spurgeon's usual straightforward manner, he proclaimed to his congregation, "In all its bearings upon scriptural truth, the evolution theory is in direct opposition to it. If God's word be true, evolution is a lie. I will not mince the matter; this is not the time for soft speaking."[211] In an 1888 sermon, Spurgeon showed the danger of this theory that could lead weak-willed believers astray:

I have seen living men carried about on biers. Here is a man who has long heard the good old-fashioned gospel; but, the other day, he met with a believer in evolution, one of the monkey-worshippers of whom I told you last Thursday night, whose father is not in heaven, but up a tree. "Oh!" said the foolish man, as he listened to the heresy-monger, "this evolution theory is a very wonderful thing," and so three or four of them bore him off on a bier, carried him away from the truth as it is in Christ.[212]

Thus, the influence of Charles Darwin and his philosophy would seep into the hearts of the church, politics, and academia alike, an influence that still pervades those environments today. Movies like *Inherit the Wind*, which took artistic license with the 1925 *Scopes* case (a.k.a., "the monkey trial") present, as Phillip E. Johnson would note, "religious fanatics who would invade a school

---

[211] Spurgeon, "Hideous Discovery," *MTP* 32:1911 (1886).
[212] Spurgeon, "Once Dead, Now Alive," *MTP* 40:2388 (1888).

classroom to persecute an inoffensive science teacher, and of a heroic defense lawyer [Clarence Darrow] who symbolizes reason itself in its endless battle against superstition."[213] Thus, Hollywood would regurgitate the notion of Darwinism being science and Christianity being superstition—a warning many gave, Spurgeon included, when Darwin's theory began to take hold in the culture's worldview.

Given the effect of this case on Darwinism, many professors gladly and gleefully accepted Darwinism not as a theory but as the only plausible explanation for the origin of all things. "All biologists, I think, would agree that evolution is the largest and most encompassing [theme] of them all. Evolution has provided the framework for life, in general, and therefore it will be the theme of this textbook."[214] Of late, men like Phillip E. Johnson, along with scientists such as Michael J. Behe in his influential book *Darwin's Black Box: The Biochemical Challenge to Evolution,* show that skeptics of Darwinism exist in the scientific realm.[215] Even so, Spurgeon warned about the effects of Darwinism and, as was his wont, he proved most prophetic.

---

[213] Johnson, *Darwin on Trial,* 4. This case sought to overturn a statute from the Tennessee legislature which symbolically prohibited the teaching of evolution (yet with an understanding that the authorities would not enforce this ban). A test case was produced by those who opposed the law when a substitute teacher named Scopes was enlisted to be the defendant. William Jennings Bryan (three-time Democratic presidential candidate) served as prosecutor. The defense lawyer, Clarence Darrow, put Bryan on the stand, seeking to undermine Bryan's Christianity and his view of the Bible—and in turn humiliated him. Though Bryan won the case, Johnson noted rightly that this "was a public relations triumph for Darwinism" (5).

[214] *The Ideas of Biology,* ix. Quoted in Morris, *The Twilight of Evolution,* 1.

[215] Behe, *Darwin's Black Box: A Biochemical Challenge to Evolution— 10th Anniversary Edition,* ix-x. In the preface, Behe lays down the concerns behind Darwin's evolutionary theory. "Yet understanding how something works is not the same as understanding how it came to be. For example, the motions of the planets in the solar system can be predicted with tremendous accuracy; however the origin of the solar system (the question of how the sun, planets, and their moons formed in the first place) is still controversial. . . . There has been virtually no attempt to account for the origin of specific, complex biomolecular systems, much less any progress."

As this chapter progresses toward evaluating the poor hermeneutics applied to those who believed in Scripture, one must recognize that Spurgeon did not take umbrage with science in general—for that is often the accusation of those who hold to Darwinism toward those who hold to Creationism. "We look up to the wondrous depths of shoreless night, and we see the starry fleet sailing along, and we believe God is their captain. We look further still, and as by the aid of science we discover the void illimitable, we believe that God dwells there, and is the infinite Creator and preserver of all things that exist and subsist."[216]

Much of science is observational, allowing each observer to bring personal biases into the process. Spurgeon believed that this type of science served as an ally in helping everyone understand more about the world God created—and helping the believer worship the Creator and His creative work even more robustly. Observing the creation rightly is critical, as is observing Scripture rightly.

Problematic Hermeneutics
in the Defense of Slavery

In American evangelicalism, especially in the American South, poor hermeneutics perpetuated a problematic view of race from none other than the Scriptures themselves. In 1861, Philip Schaff, in his book *Slavery and the Bible: A Tract for the Times*, taught that Ham (recorded in Genesis 9 as one of the sons of Noah who was cursed for seeing his drunken father naked and reacted dishonorably about the event to his brothers), who bore Canaan, "represents the idolatrous and servile races."[217] Schaff goes on,

The curse was occasioned by gross indecency and profane irreverence to the aged Noah. It was inflicted upon Canaan, the youngest of the four sons of Ham, either because this was, according to an ancient Jewish tradition, the real offender, and Ham merely the reporter of the face, or more probably because

---

[216] Spurgeon, "The Great Supreme," *MTP* 7:367 (1856).
[217] Schaff, *Slavery and the Bible: A Tract for the Times*, 6–7.

he made sport of his grandfather's shame when seen and revealed by Ham to his brothers, and was the principal heir of the irreverence and impiety of his father… Whether we connect it with his ancient prophecy or not, it is simply a fact which no one can deny, that the negro to this day is a servant of servants in our own midst.[218]

Many Christian believers in the American South widely accepted this interpretation by justifying their involvement in the institution of slavery. Mark Noll observed,

The main reason those alternative hermeneutics failed on the question of slavery was the widespread commonsense [*sic*] consensus about race. Although the Bible and race was never the same question as the Bible and slavery, only African Americans perceived this reality clearly at the time....On slavery, exegetes stood for a commonsense [sic] reading of the Bible. On race, exegetes forsook the Bible and relied on common sense. Intuitive judgments on American slavery were therefore sanctified by the culture's intuitive biblicism and literally *colored* by the culture's intuitive racism.[219]

This frustrated men like Frederick Douglass who defended slavery from the Scriptures. Yet, as he himself referred to the Scripture with his hermeneutical sloppiness, Douglass would travel down a trail that debunked the church and even the Scriptures themselves. "The same Book which is full of the Gospel of Liberty to one race, is crowded with arguments in justification of slavery of another. Those who shout and rejoice over the progress of Liberty in Italy, would mob down, pray and preach down Liberty at home as an unholy and hateful thing."[220]

Yet, did the Scriptures justify this type of slavery? Spurgeon did not believe so, saying,

---

[218] Schaff, *Slavery*, 6–7.

[219] Noll, *America's God: From Jonathan Edwards to Abraham Lincoln*, 417–18.

[220] Frederick Douglass, "The Pro-Slavery Mob and the Pro-Slavery Ministry," 417–18.

Some American divines seem to regard it, indeed, with wonderful complacency. They have so accustomed themselves to wrap it up in soft phrases that they lose sight of its real character. They call it a "peculiar institution," until they forget in what its peculiarity consists. It is, indeed, a peculiar institution, just as the Devil is a peculiar angel, and as hell is a peculiarly hot place. For my part, I hold such miserable tampering with sin in abhorrence, and can hold no communion of any sort with those who are guilty of it.[221]

While the sloppy hermeneutics came from particular "divines" from the American South who sought to derive their slave-based practices from Scripture, Spurgeon used the phrase "wonderful complacency" due to a culture used to this institution. Spurgeon stated he "can hold no communion", which infers that he did not consider them followers of Christ, no matter how much they said otherwise. And, adding insult to injury, Spurgeon believed Lincoln was sent by God to rescue those in slavery:

When the negro slave had borne long years of bondage, and hope of deliverance seemed far away, it was God that gave an Abraham Lincoln, who led the nation onward till "Emancipation" flamed upon its banners. Long before, when England, free in every corner of it, yet held slaves in its colonies, it was God that gave Wilberforce, and raised him up to plead in Parliament the rights of men, till the command went forth.[222]

How could Spurgeon, who preached from the Scriptures, stand so strongly against slavery if slavery was indeed justified from Scripture? Does not the Bible teach that slavery is permissible, especially in the Old Testament? Does not slavery exist among God's people in the Pentateuch and beyond? Spurgeon received this question in his day as well,

---

[221] Fant and Pinson, *20 Centuries of Great Preaching*, 6. Quoted in Estep.

[222] Spurgeon, "Certain Singular Subjects," *MTP* 29 (1873).

The slavery which existed amongst the ancient Jews was a very different thing from that which has disgraced humanity in modern times; and it ought also to be remembered that Moses did not institute slavery in any shape; the laws concerning it were made on purpose to repress it, to confine it within very narrow bounds, and ultimately to put an end to it. It was like the law of divorce: Moses found that law, and he knew that the people were so deeply rooted in it that it could not be forbidden; and therefore, as Jesus tells us, Moses, because of the hardness of their hearts, suffered them to put away their wives. And so, I may say, because of the hardness of their hearts he suffered them still to retain persons in servitude, but he made the laws very stringent, so as almost to prevent it.[223]

Those using the Scriptures to advocate slavery in modern times would do well to hear from Spurgeon: "Moses did not institute slavery in any shape; the laws concerning it were made on purpose to repress it, to confine it."[224] Yet, like in the American South and many other places where slavery existed and was so much ingrained in their respective culture, they could not bring themselves to uproot this practice from their culture. The mistake the American Southern slaveowners made was only seeing the description of slavery in the Scriptures as a prescription for slavery in their society. What they could not see was their hardness of heart that allowed this "description" of this practice to continue. Thus, Spurgeon's conviction that all are image bearers of God informed with a zealous flame that slavery (especially race-based slavery) should be vanquished from the earth. All who believe this practice is appropriate and, given the sloppy hermeneutics that surrounded the subject, believe that God accepts this practice must repent:

For nations there is a weighing time. National sins demand national punishments. The whole history of God's dealings with mankind proves that though a nation may go on in wickedness it may multiply its oppressions; it may abound in bloodshed,

---

[223] Spurgeon, "The Ear Bored with the Awl," *MTP* 20:1174 (1874).
[224] Spurgeon, "The Ear Bored with the Awl."

tyranny, and war, but an hour of retribution draweth nigh....There is no God in heaven if the iniquity of slavery go unpunished. There is no God existing in heaven above if the cry of the negro do not bring down a red hail of blood upon the nation that still holds the black man in slavery.[225]

Efforts were made to get Spurgeon to tone down his remarks on slavery in the American South. He was warned by friends and newspaper editors alike that his printed sermons would no longer be circulated in America if he kept up his attack. One newspaper seethed, "If the Pharisaical author should ever show himself in these parts, we trust that a stout cord may speedily find its way around his eloquent throat."[226] American publishers soon eliminated all his references to slavery. Because of this editing, some readers in America wondered if Spurgeon had changed his mind. Henry Ward Beecher declared that Spurgeon had not altered his opinions and had no responsibility for the omissions made in his sermons. Sadly, the ones who struggled most with Spurgeon's views were those from fellow Baptists in the United States.

Baptists' Reaction to
Spurgeon's View on Slavery

When evaluating the American Baptists, Thomas Kidd and Barry Hankins observed: "As Baptists spread throughout the American South in the early nineteenth century, so did slavery. Some white Baptists in the Revolutionary era had condemned Christian slave-owning, but over time most white Baptists in the South made peace with the institution, whether they owned slaves or not."[227]

---

[225] Spurgeon, "Scales of Judgment," *MTP* 5:257 (1859).

[226] *The Southern Reporter and Daily Commercial Courier* [April 10, 1860]).

[227] Kidd and Hankins, *Baptists in America*, 98. They continue, "This trend accelerated as Baptists helped fashion a new kind of cultural and religious establishment, especially in the southern states of the Atlantic seaboard, and many Baptist elites came to own slaves. Yet the issue of human bondage festered as the small but boisterous antislavery movement won over some white northern evangelicals. Everyday pressure against slavery came most directly from black Baptists themselves."

Sadly, when many evangelical churches decided that the issue of slavery was too divisive, they determined that slavery and emancipation were more political discussions than religious ones.[228] By relegating this issue to the politicians of the time, they unwittingly took the opposite course of William Wilberforce, whose political leanings showed slavery as a religious discussion as well. Thus, when the American Baptists in the South began to interact with a fellow Baptist in England named Charles Haddon Spurgeon, his views on their favored institution were received with a blistering reaction.

While much has been said about Spurgeon's view of racism about the cultural moorings of the day, a deeper look into the theological groundings of Spurgeon's preaching is in order. Though Spurgeon never attended college or seminary, his thirst for knowledge and his desire to rightly interpret the Word of truth (2 Tm 2:15) led him to become a theologian of the first order. His beliefs translated into actions—yet the Scriptures planted those seeds.

Theology that Informed
Spurgeon's Hatred of Racism

Spurgeon's hatred of racism did not stem solely from a sociological perspective or upbringing but stood anchored first in the Scriptures. Spurgeon's theological underpinnings derived from Scripture set the course for all his preaching and interactions with church and culture alike. The doctrines most formative for Spurgeon were the conviction of the *imago Dei*, the adoption of the believer, election, and God's lack of partiality. Each of these doctrines from Scripture worked together in implementing Christ's command to love one's neighbor as oneself. Spurgeon's overall theological contention was that the gospel of Jesus Christ changed lives:

> We have only to preach the living gospel, and the whole of it, to meet the whole of the evils of the times. The gospel, if it were

---

[228] Najar M., "'Meddling with Emancipation': Baptists, Authority, and the Rift over Slavery in the Upper South."

fully received through the whole earth, would purge away all slavery and all war, and put down all drunkenness and all social evils; in fact, you cannot conceive a moral curse which it would not remove; and even physical evils, since many of them arise incidentally from sin, would be greatly mitigated, and some of them for ever abolished. The spirit of the gospel, causing attention to be given to all that concerns our neighbor's welfare, would promote sanitary and social reforms, and so the leaves of the tree which are for the healing of the nations would work their beneficial purpose.[229]

The *Imago Dei*

Spurgeon held strongly to the doctrine of the image of God—that all of humanity are image bearers of God, without question. This doctrine permeated Spurgeon's life, preaching and ministry, informing his views on racism. This doctrine is the foundation of how Spurgeon sought to influence believers and countrymen alike toward the Creator's design and intentions for humanity's relationship with itself. Lewis Drummond noted, "Spurgeon advocated the breaking down of barriers between the classes, but not the eradication of the classes themselves, thus merging all people into a classless society. He contended that each rank or stratum of society ought to know and keep its divinely appointed place, yet be open to one another."[230]

Spurgeon preached not only to his congregation but to all his fellow Englishmen:

Everyone [sic] of you (Englishmen) seek to cultivate a generous spirit toward his neighbor. Let not the rich oppress the poor; let not the poor envy the rich, let us all pull together heart and soul, as being brothers of one race. My dear friends, let us not think that our national prosperity must always endure through the intrinsic excellence of our constitution. No, our confidence must be in our God, and, under God, in ourselves; in our honesty, in

---

[229] Spurgeon, *An All-Around Ministry* (Apollo, PA: Ichthus Publications, 2014), 80.

[230] Drummond, *Spurgeon*, 402.

our integrity; in our generous sympathy with one another; in keeping of each rank in its own place; in the non-intrusion of any man into another man's rights; in respect to property and respect to labor, in respect to learning and respect to manhood ... capitals in reform, but not in revolution; in radicalism, so far as to destroy everything that is radically wrong; and in conservatism so far as to conserve every particle of right.[231]

While the themes in the previous quote will also arise later in this work regarding the subject of religious liberty and conscience, the transferrable principle from Spurgeon is clear: God has placed each segment of humanity in its place for his sovereign purpose and glory. Spurgeon's absorption of Jesus' command to love one's neighbor as oneself bled over into every possible aspect of society. The operative phrase in this quote is, "cultivate a generous spirit toward his neighbor." Spurgeon believed that once a country leaves God's design, that country's days are numbered. Racism, along with any other worldview that sees one group as superior to another, does not belong in a country's ecosystem, especially in a country that claims to be "under God." Sadly, these countries drift due to the problematic hermeneutics preached in churches that kowtow to cultural leanings rather than standing firm on the precepts of Scripture.

In 1872, Spurgeon preached on the difficult doctrine of predestination. While the scope of this work does not delve into Spurgeon's staunch Calvinism, this sermon discusses the doctrine of humanity as image bearers of God who, because of Adam, fell under the curse of sin and death. "Man was originally made in the image of God, but by sin, he has defaced that image, and now we who are born into this world are fashioned, not in the heavenly image of God, but in the earthly image of the fallen Adam. 'We have born,' says the Apostle, in the First Epistle to the Corinthians, 'the image of the earthy.'"[232] This sinful corruption of the soul clouded humanity's view of the heavenly Savior as well as humanity's movement as an image bearer of God.

---

[231] Spurgeon, *Poland*, 23. Quoted in Drummond, 402.
[232] Spurgeon, "Glorious Predestination," *MTP* 18:1043 (1872).

As mentioned earlier, Darwinism undermined this doctrine by denying the Creator's work in the advent of humanity into the world. This philosophy saddened Spurgeon greatly for all that those who hold to this worldview would miss when encountering the reality of the Creator's majesty:

> All God's works praise him, whether they be magnificent or minute, they all discover the wisdom, the power, and the benevolence of their Creator... The most wicked of men have been obliged to acknowledge that there must be a Creator, when they have heard that marvelous voice sounding through the sky. Men of the stoutest nerve and boldest blasphemy have become the weakest of creatures, when God has manifested himself in the mighty whirlwind or in the storm.[233]

This excerpt came from an 1856 sermon, three years before the publication of Darwin's *Origin of the Species*. As mentioned previously, Darwin's triumph arose thanks to a desire to show the origin of all things without referring to or relying on religious narratives for an explanation. For with a Creator who made humanity in His image would come the responsibility of the image bearer to surrender to the Creator. "Should not the creature be submissive to the Creator, to whom it owes its existence, without whom it had never been, and without whose continuous good pleasure it would at once cease to be?"[234] Without this Creator, the origin and continuation of life would be impossible. Thus, all humans are image bearers of God, regardless of gender, race, or societal status. Spurgeon preached in 1889:

> The Lord had made man in his own image; he had created him a remarkable being of united matter and spirit; but man made a revolt from him, so that "it repented the Lord that he had made man on the earth." When the Lord looks upon our race at this

---

[233] Spurgeon, "The Majestic Voice," *NPSP* 2:87 (1856).
[234] Spurgeon, "Unconditional Surrender," *MTP* 22:1276 (1882).

moment, he cannot take satisfaction in creatures who have made themselves so vile.[235]

This excerpt is important because Spurgeon noted that God looked at "our race," not *the* races.

Understanding how humanity is made in the image of God was of critical importance to Spurgeon's ministry and anthropology that, as this chapter will show, would feed Spurgeon's gospel message as well. In an 1861 sermon, Spurgeon leaned into the longing God placed in all humans to gravitate to the One in whose image they were made:

> If Eden had been a Sahara, a howling desert, the truly spiritual mind would long to have it back again for one reason, namely, that there man was in the image of his Maker....All the losses we sustained by Adam's ruin were very little, compared with that great loss of the likeness and undying, like the God whose image Adam bore, we might well have endured to have the earth sterile and barren; and all the pains had still retained the image of God.[236]

While all of humanity was made in God's likeness, Spurgeon repeatedly reminded his congregation and readers that only through Christ could one fully become an image of God. Spurgeon's ministry promoted the notion that Christ is the perfect representation of the Father. "Man can never be so expressly the image of the Father as Jesus is, for he is in a mysterious sense the only begotten Son of God."[237] This came as a result of the distress of those who used other images in their worship, using language that made Spurgeon's understandings of the Scriptures quite clear. He preached that the Spirit of God led Christians to comprehend the sinfulness and idolatry that hid in their hearts. "He leads us into the abominable chambers of imagery concealed within our fallen

---

[235] Spurgeon, "The Father's Dying Love to His Son," *MTP* 35:2117 (1889).

[236] Spurgeon, "Portraits of Christ," *MTP* 7:355 (1861).

[237] Spurgeon, "The Leading of the Spirit, the Secret Token of the Sons of God," *MTP* 21:1220 (1875).

nature, unfastens door after door and sets open before our enlightened eyes the secret places polluted with idols and loathsome images portrayed upon the wall."[238]

Spurgeon assured his congregation that God made us at Creation in His image—and thus sent Christ to make His people fully in His image, body, and soul. "The image of Christ is the Spirit's great work in us. On that day, when we are regenerated, the new man is put into us; now in what image is the new man? It is the image of the one who created him ... renewed in the image of Christ."[239]

Adoption

Spurgeon believed the New Testament's admonition and belief that anyone, regardless of race, gender, or any demographic, could be chosen as a follower of Christ—a son of God, one who would inherit the riches of Christ. "Now, faith is the mark of sonship in all who have it, whoever they may be, for 'ye are all the children of God by faith in Christ Jesus' (Gal 3:26). If you are believing in Jesus, whether you are Jew or Gentile, bond or free, you are a son of God." [240] In an 1861 sermon, in his usual illustrative manner, Spurgeon drove home the nature of adoption to whoever would receive Christ:

If a king should adopt any into his family, it would likely be the son of his lords—at any rate, some child of respectable parentage; he would scarce take the son of some common felon, or some gipsy child, to adopt him into his family; but God, in this case, has taken the very worst to be his children. The saints of God all confess they are the last persons they should ever have dreamed he would have chosen.[241]

Spurgeon's theology informed all he preached, especially on topics such as slavery. In an 1861 sermon (the same year that the

---

[238] Spurgeon, "The Leading of the Spirit."

[239] Spurgeon, "Portraits of Christ," *MTP* 7:355 (1861).

[240] Spurgeon, "Adoption, the Spirit, and the Cry," *MTP* 24:1435 (1878).

[241] Spurgeon, "Adoption," *MTP* 7:360 (1861).

American Civil War began), he preached a moving sermon on the important biblical topic of redemption—but not in an academic way that merely described the definition, but more about how this glorious doctrine changes the heart toward God and others, even those in the continent of Africa:

> Redemption is a word which has gladdened many ears, when there was no heavenly sound in its blessed chime. Apart from any theological use of it, the word is a very sweet one, and has been melodious to many hearts. In those days when piracy was carried on continually along the coast of Africa, when our fellow Christian subjects were caught by corsairs, and carried away captive, you can well understand how the burdened soul of the manacled slave, chained to the oar of his galley, was gladdened by the hope that possibly there would be redemption. His cruel master, who had forced him into his possession, would not willingly emancipate him; but a rumour came, that in some distant nation they had raised a sum of money to purchase the freedom of slaves—that some wealthy merchant had dedicated of his substance to buy back his fellow-countrymen; that the king himself upon his throne had promised to give a liberal redemption that the captives among the Moors might return to their homes. Truly I can suppose the hours would run happily along, and the dreariness of their toil would be assuaged, when once that word "redemption" had sounded in their ears.[242]

Redemption's movement must not stay within the realms of the spiritual or the mystical. The illustration Spurgeon used was a timely one. Though he hearkened back to the days in England when the slave trade was robust, he also recognized that a consequent war was taking place over this very institution. This, along with other sermons even more pointed, would create a breach between him and his white evangelical slaveholding brothers (a term Spurgeon would not use in describing those who called themselves Christians *and* possessed other dark-skinned image bearers in chains), for he once said,

---

[242] Spurgeon, "Plenteous Redemption," *MTP* 7:351 (1861).

I do from my inmost soul detest slavery ... and although I commune at the Lord's table with men of all creeds, yet with a slave-holder I have no fellowship of any sort or kind. Whenever one has called upon me, I have considered it my duty to express my detestation of his wickedness, and I would as soon think of receiving a murderer into my church ... as a man stealer.[243]

Spurgeon's theology regarding the adoption of his image bearers into spiritual sons would not allow Spurgeon to reconcile himself into advocating slavery among those naming the name of Christ.

God's Sovereign Election
in Salvation

Spurgeon often preached that "with regard to adoption, I believe we were predestined thereunto in eternity; but I do think there are some points with regard to adoption which will not allow me to consider the act of adoption to have been completed in eternity."[244] Spurgeon believed in the sovereign work of God in electing His people to salvation, begun in eternity past but applied in the here and now. He adopted them based on His choosing, not the choice of the adopted. At a mere twenty-one years old, Spurgeon knew that many approached this doctrine with an "inveterate prejudice"[245] and as one that is "most frequently disregarded and discarded."[246] In many pulpits, Spurgeon noted that this "would be reckoned a high sin and treason" on which to preach.[247] And, as such, God did not choose whom He chose due to any attribute they may hold:

Observe, then, that when the Son of God determined to die for men, he views them as ungodly, and far from God by wicked works. In casting his eye over our race he did not say, "Here and there I see spirits of nobler mould, pure, truthful, truth-seeking, brave, disinterested, and just; and therefore, because of these

---

[243] H. Golden Pike, *The Life and Work of Charles Haddon Spurgeon*, 33.
[244] Spurgeon, "Adoption."
[245] Spurgeon, "Election," *MTP* 1:41–42 (1855).
[246] Spurgeon, "Election."
[247] Spurgeon, "Election."

choice ones, I will die for this fallen race." No; but looking on them all, he whose judgment is infallible returned this verdict, "They are all gone out of the way; they are together become unprofitable; there is none that doeth good, no, not one."[248]

This quote from an 1874 sermon must capture the attention of one working to absorb Spurgeon's gospel-centered ethic on racial matters. Spurgeon had long established that, just as no one is saved by their good works, no one is saved by their oppressed condition:

> If you conceive that by your good works you shall enter heaven, never was there a more fell delusion, and you shall find at the last great day, that your hopes were worthless, and that, like sear leaves from the autumn trees, your noblest doings shall be blown away, or kindled into a flame within you yourselves must suffer for ever. Take heed of your good works; get them after faith, but remember, the way to be saved is simply to believe in Jesus Christ.[249]

In the context of this chapter, although colonial states may shake the shackles of Spurgeon's British Empire and slaves may become emancipated in the Southern plantations thanks to the pen of President Lincoln or the gun of the Northern soldier, this should not stand as evidence of God's *salvific* work—the work of common grace, yes! No condition or service on earth rescues anyone from their spiritual brokenness outside the atoning work of Christ. To suggest anything else? Spurgeon would have none of it because the Scriptures would have none of it.

More to the point of this section, Spurgeon preached clearly that God would choose a people from the four corners of the earth. God's election is all of grace, is not partial, and is a "work now is that of gathering. There was a time when it was scattering. Man built the tower of Babel, which was intended to be the centre of unity....Man's centre is not God's centre, and therefore he confounded their language, and scattered them into the nations, by

---

[248] Spurgeon, "For Whom Did Christ Die?" *MTP* 20:1191 (1874).
[249] Spurgeon, "Faith" *NPSP* 3:107 (1856).

whom the whole earth has been inhabited."[250] Babel served as a place where humanity sought to exert their supposed-sovereign power over the earth. The divisions and distinctions that exist on the earth from an earthly aspect originated here for their protection. Their unity became confusion, for God scattered them—but that would not be the end of the story. "Now the Lord is gathering together in one the children of God which are scattered abroad. His Son Jesus Christ hath descended and dwelt among us, working out our redemption, and now, exalted in the highest heavens, he is God's appointed centre of his people."[251]

Spurgeon echoed the heart of the Savior by making no distinction of race in the gathering of God's people to Himself. The end goal of God is to bring His people to Christ. Nothing will last that man makes. "Man may erect his structures and think they may last forever, but the Tower of Babel has crumbled, and the very Pyramids bear signs of ruin. Nothing which man has made is everlasting, because he cannot ensure it against decay."[252]

Thus, Christ sends His elect into the world to preach to all nations to rescue the elect rather than make one lazy in the effort. "The fact is, the most zealous, the most earnest, and the most successful of men, have been those Who have held this truth, and therefore it cannot be true that this tends to damp our energies or thwart our zeal."[253] Rather,

It is our anxious endeavour to be clean as men chosen to bear the vessels of the Lord. It is our hearty prayer that in season and out of season we may labour for the winning of men's souls, knowing that to God's churches is committed the work of gathering in those sheep who are not of his fold, but who must be brought in, that there may be one flock and one Shepherd.[254]

---

[250] Spurgeon, "Others to be Gathered," *MTP* 24:1437 (1878).

[251] Spurgeon, "Others to be Gathered."

[252] Spurgeon, "The Blood of the Everlasting Covenant," *NPSP* 5:277 (1859).

[253] Spurgeon, "Effects of Sound Doctrine," *NPSP* 6:324 (1860).

[254] Spurgeon, "Effects of Sound Doctrine."

God used His elect to gather in and reverse the travesty that happened at Babel. Babel sought to exalt self, yet the doctrine of election exalted God in his mercy as He sought to protect His creation from their own selfish and ultimately destructive ambition. "Our heart adores and wonders as we think of the election of God. As we rise in the assurance of the divine choice, we sink in our valuation of ourselves."[255]

Spurgeon also contended that the doctrine of election "fosters a feeling of holy brotherhood."[256] This insight escaped so many when broaching this doctrine. In preaching this sermon, Spurgeon nailed the glories of this doctrine in one of his most beautiful and thoughtful excerpts:

> How beautiful it is to see the learned and the illiterate, the great and the lowly, made one family by the grace of God! It is marvelous what power this has had in the Christian church; and I pray its power may be felt more and more until everything like caste and class is abolished in the church of God, and we shall become brethren indeed and of a truth. As the chosen of God, our names are written in the same book, we are redeemed with the same blood, we are called by the same Spirit, we are quickened by the same life, and hope soon to meet in the same heaven. This is the truest confederation, the union of hearts in the common Lord. As the elect of God we break away from the world, but we come together in one body in Christ.[257]

Notice how Spurgeon brought out particular groups of people: Learned and illiterate, the great and the lowly. And then, to the point of this section, "Until everything like caste and class is abolished in the church of God, and we shall become brethren indeed and of a truth."[258] The doctrine of election is an important tenet of theology that fueled Spurgeon's preaching and activism regarding race (among other issues).

---

[255] Spurgeon, "David Dancing before the Ark Because of His Election," *MTP* 34:2031 (1888).

[256] Spurgeon, "David Dancing."

[257] Spurgeon, "David Dancing."

[258] Spurgeon, "David Dancing."

God's Lack of Partiality

In addressing the issue of racism, Spurgeon reflected the biblical admonition of God's refusal to show partiality—a common thread throughout this entire project. As addressed in the previous chapter, Christians must not show partiality based on nationality or patriotic residue. Wilberforce's theological convictions sought to eliminate the division between inferior and superior notions among the races; Darwin sought to fan the flame. Yet, Spurgeon's greatest influence was not Wilberforce, but Jesus himself.

In a sermon on the Parable of the Good Samaritan (Luke 10:25–37), Spurgeon addressed the criticism some preachers face when they start preaching on moral teachings rather than sticking to "the gospel." In this parable, when the lawyer asked about eternal life, Jesus prodded him about the greatest commandments. When the lawyer answered, in essence, to love God with all one has and to love one's neighbor as oneself, Jesus congratulated him on answering correctly. However, the lawyer had not finished his query. "And who is my neighbor?" which was asked to justify himself. Here, Jesus connected one's eternal standing before God with how one treated his neighbor, i.e., their fellow image bearers. "Jesus tells us over and over again the manner in which we are to live towards our fellow-men, and he lays great stress upon the love which should shine through the Christian character....Let it never be forgotten that what the law demands of us the gospel really produces in us."[259]

To those who believed that slavery was exclusively a political issue (as was said in England and in the American South to avoid the hard question among the churches), Jesus set the course for all churches. Christ's admonition to love one's neighbor as oneself settled the argument once and for all. No partiality comes from God, and no partiality must come from His people.

Another aspect of God's lack of partiality is that of sin and salvation. In an 1882 sermon, Spurgeon preached on the plague of the firstborn while Israel was enslaved in Egypt. God preserved the Israelites as the "angel of vengeance sped through every street of

---

[259] Spurgeon, "The Good Samaritan," *MTP* 23:1360 (1877).

Pharaoh's domain and slew the firstborn of all the land, both of men and of cattle."[260] Spurgeon used this to remind the believer about God's vengeance against sin toward them, but that a way of deliverance existed. Spurgeon then drove the point home,

> Memory may drop all else from her enfeebled grasp, but this is graven on the palms of her hands. The mode of our deliverance is before us in the type as Moses describes it. The angel could not be restrained, his wing could not be bound, and his sword could not be sheathed: he must go forth, and he must smite. He must smite us among the rest, for sin was upon us, and there must be no partiality: "the soul that sinneth it shall die." But do you remember when you discovered God's new way, his blessed ordinance by which, without abrogating the destroying law, he brought in a glorious saving clause by which we were delivered?[261]

No matter one's gender, race, or station in life, "the soul that sinneth it shall die" (Ezek 18:20). God created all humanity as image bearers. All humanity has fallen in sin and come short of the glory of God (Rom 3:23). Sin shows no partiality, but neither does God's grace. In relation to the previous section about God's sovereign election, this may demonstrate that God is indeed partial. Spurgeon contended,

> Some seem to fancy that Jesus is their servant, at their beck and call; and they talk about his salvation as though he ought to give it, and they could claim it for themselves and all mankind. If we speak about the sovereign choice of some unto eternal life, they begin chattering about injustice and partiality: as if any guilty man had a right to anything from the Lord of glory, except the dreadful right to be punished for his sins.[262]

---

[260] Spurgeon, "The Beginning of Months," *MTP* 28:1637 (1882).
[261] Spurgeon, "The Beginning of Months."
[262] Spurgeon, "Self Low, but Christ High," 36:2161 (1890).

Yet all are in sin, and as such "we have no claim on God. If he chooses to save us, it must be of his own free grace."[263]

Conclusion

This chapter aimed to develop a gospel-centered ethic toward the vulnerable regarding racism. In examining Spurgeon's preaching, a case has been made that Spurgeon's influences and theology strengthened his convictions regarding the devaluing of someone merely due to his race or the color of his skin. Though the English and American cultures began embracing a godless origin narrative that most outside the church and many inside would, Spurgeon perpetually pointed to the authority of Scripture for direction.

The next chapter delves into the areas of religious liberty and conscience. What did Spurgeon believe was the role of government in connection to the church? Did the citizens and churches have a freedom to follow their consciences as they pleased?

---

[263] Spurgeon, "Self Low."

Spurgeon's Ethic
on Religious Liberty

Charles Haddon Spurgeon stood in a long line of Christians who defended religious liberty. He did so believing that authorities who restricted this freedom committed tyranny against their citizens. As Spurgeon preached fervently about the priority of a Christian's heavenly citizenship over his earthly citizenship (Chapter Three), this section shows how Spurgeon wrestled with that relationship, just like every other generation of Christians.

Spurgeon sought to help his congregation and the surrounding culture understand the nature of religious freedom that existed under the shadow of the Anglican Church in their marriage of the political and the religious. As Robert Louis Wilken rightly noted, "Religious freedom rests on a simple truth: religious faith is an inward disposition of the mind and heart and for that reason cannot be coerced."[264] This is along the lines of fourth-century theologian Tertullian (AD 155–220) in his *Apology* around AD 197:

> Let one man worship God, another Jupiter; let one lift suppliant hands to the heavens, another to the altar of Fides; let one—if you choose to take this view of it—count in prayer the clouds, and another the ceiling panels; let one consecrate his own life to his God, and another that of a goat. For see that you do not give a further ground for the charge of irreligion, by taking away religious liberty, and forbidding free choice of deity, so that I may no longer worship according to my inclination, but

---

[264] Robert Louis Wilken, *Liberty in the Things of God*, Kindle Location 55.

am compelled to worship against it. Not even a human being would care to have unwilling homage rendered him.[265]

Spurgeon fought against this coercion from the Established Church, a battle fought on many fronts throughout church history.

This chapter examines several of Spurgeon's sermons to demonstrate his strong beliefs concerning religious liberty and freedom of conscience. He helped his contemporary culture in the latter half of the nineteenth century navigate through the troublesome waters of having those liberties threatened and taken away. This chapter also discusses Spurgeon's dissenter roots which formulated his views on the rights of conscience; Spurgeon's clarifying remarks as to what religious liberty is not; from whom Spurgeon sought religious freedom; how these rights affected the entire nation; and how these freedoms help the Christian message move among the citizenries. This chapter also demonstrates the cost that Spurgeon paid for his convictions in this manner, and how the freedom he sought and defended would be used in his own denomination to pursue problematic doctrines that infiltrated Baptist work. The concluding chapter will construct a gospel-centered ethic for those seeking freedom of conscience in worship.

What Religious Liberty is Not

Spurgeon did not believe freedom of religion meant freedom *from* religious influence. Spurgeon frequently addressed this topic in his day. In an 1889 sermon, Spurgeon preached unequivocally about the tyranny that came not from the political authorities but citizens themselves and railed against those who went into their workplaces and collectively mocked the

> solitary Christian youth when you each one have your jibe, when you give him what you call 'chaff,' which is sport to you, but cruel enough to be death to him, did it never occur to you that it was a most cowardly thing, and altogether unworthy of you, that ten, twenty, thirty, forty, fifty, should all set upon one? What if

---

[265] Tertullian, *Apology*, 47.

a man does believe in religion? Has he not the right to do so if he likes? Some of you who talk so much about freedom are the biggest bullies in the world; you boast loudly of religious liberty, but to you it means liberty to be irreligious. Surely I have as much right to worship Christ as you have to despise him; and if my views of religion should seem to you to be peculiar, yet, if peculiar, have I not as good reason to hold them as you have to reject them?"[266]

For Spurgeon, freedom of conscience (especially when addressing religious conscience) was a matter for which plain-spokenness and boldness were a necessity. The war on this freedom took place in politics, on the streets, in the workplaces, in the homes—every place where opinions and peer pressure could be leveraged. Spurgeon believed this was of utmost seriousness—he held that these persecutors would find themselves descendants of the same company as those who persecuted Christ:

I speak thus plainly because I know of many, many cases where, if men were men at all, they would cease to persecute Christians, seeing that they persecute one or two wherever they can if they themselves happen to be in the majority. Think of this lot of howling dogs around this one gentle Lamb of God, the Christ who had never even a hard word for them, whose mightiest weapon was silence and patience; think of him surrounded by all these men of war from their youth up, these Roman legionaries with their imperial eagles. It was a cruel shame. The more there were of them, the meaner it was of them thus, as a whole band, to gather together to mock the Saviour.[267]

Spurgeon helped his congregation and the surrounding culture know what religious liberty does not entail.

Belief in religious liberty does not mean a belief that all religions are equal, even as many (Spurgeon included) fight for everyone's right to follow their conscience in full religious freedom.

---

[266] Spurgeon, "The Whole Band Against Christ," *MTP* 39:2333 (1889).

[267] Spurgeon, "The Whole Band Against Christ."

Again, religious liberty means no coercion from the state over the consciences of their citizens. Evangelicals still have a responsibility to compel others to receive the gospel of Christ and, at the same time, demonstrate the deficiencies of other religions in providing justification for sins and being rigorous in sharing the truth. For instance, in an 1873 sermon, Spurgeon noted how many other religions were experiencing growth among their people, yet Christians remained apathetic. Spurgeon desired that Christians would use the freedom they had to share the gospel with others:

> What a disgrace it is that Christians should be so indifferent to the spread of truth in these days! There has been lately a revival amongst Mahometans; we had all thought that the crescent was waning, and that Mussulmen would never endeavour to make converts again. Instead thereof there appears to have been in many parts a singular awakening of the old enthusiasm which marked the early days of Islam. What, and shall the false prophet command the zeal of his followers and shall not the Son of God possess the souls of his people? Let it not be said the Christians are cold.[268]

Spurgeon did not shy away from identifying false religions and how they could send souls astray into hell itself, for he believed that the concept of religious liberty allowed him to do so:

> But you say, "How are these idolatrous systems to be cast down?" God could do it in an hour if he pleased. Religion never moves by years and weeks. Even false religions grow like mushrooms; much more true ones. False religions attained colossal proportion in a very few years. Take the case of Mahommedanism—the new-born faith of Islam became the religion of millions in an incredible short period and if a false religion could spread so quickly, shall not a true one run along like fire amidst the stubble, when God shall speak the word? Clouds are but "dust of his feet."[269]

---

[268] Spurgeon, "The Christian's Great Business," *MTP* 19:1130 (1873).
[269] Spurgeon, "What are the Clouds? *MTP* 1:36 (1855).

In an 1888 sermon, Spurgeon reminded his congregation once again that he "...believe[s] in the fullest religious liberty, and that conscience owes allegiance to none but God: but I speak of principles: holiness cannot endure sin, righteousness cannot bear injustice, and truth cannot consort with error. 'What concord hath Christ with Belial?'"[270]

Spurgeon saw no "concord" (i.e., harmony) with "Belial," with Belial being the Church of England—a conviction that he held along with many others who clung to the foundation of their dissenting brothers and sisters.

Spurgeon's Dissenter Roots

In an 1875 sermon on Psalm 45:16, Spurgeon paid homage to his spiritual forebears. "In every effort for civil and religious liberty, our fathers were to the front. In the utterance of those divine truths which have made tyrants and priests quake for fear, they have been among the boldest."[271] Spurgeon's home life, as Estep notes, "reflected the devotional life of Victorian England's Nonconformity."[272] Soon after Spurgeon became a Christian, he joined with the Baptists—a denomination of Protestants who are the "fathers" to whom Spurgeon referred in this sermon. Growing up in a family of paedobaptist Congregationalists, Spurgeon became convinced of believer's baptism after a diligent and thorough search of the Scriptures. A well-known account is often told that soon after Spurgeon's baptism was scheduled, his mother was sorrowful that

---

[270] Spurgeon, "Jesus Known by Personal Revelation," *MTP* 34:2041 (1888). Spurgeon also noted, "Some say that thou art John the Baptist: some, Elias; and others, Jeremias, or one of the prophets." Error is multiform; truth is one. A thousand lies will live together, and tolerate each other, especially at this time, when errorists are all crying out, "Cast in thy lot with us; let us all have one purse." A thousand false gods will stand together in the Pantheon; but if the ark of the true God enters Dagon's temple, Dagon must come down on his face and be dashed to pieces. Jehovah is God alone, and will not brook a rival. Truth is of necessity intolerant of error."

[271] Spurgeon, "The Unbroken Line of True Nobles," *MTP* 21:1260 (1875).

[272] Estep, "The Making of a Prophet: An Introduction to Charles Haddon Spurgeon," *Baptist History and Heritage* 19:4 (1987), 4.

Charles would seek out believer's baptism, exclaiming that she did not pray for him to become a Baptist. His response: "Ah, mother! The Lord has answered your prayer with His usual bounty, and given you exceeding abundantly above what you asked or thought."[273] While this playful response belied the significant ecclesiastical break from Spurgeon's childhood, it also set him on a course that cut against the grain of political and religious authorities that affected everyday life in England. Yet the course Spurgeon chose to walk was part of the historical trajectory set by Baptists for generations.

Baptist historian Gregory Wills succinctly summarizes how Spurgeon's denomination led the way in religious liberty both in the culture and in the life of the church itself:

> Baptists championed the rights of conscience and private judgment in the interpretation of scripture, but people had these rights, they believed, as citizens of the state, not as members of the churches. The state had no right to inflict civil or criminal penalties for religious opinions, but churches had every right to inflict spiritual penalties for erroneous beliefs. The authority to censure members for wrong doctrine was a matter of both freedom and unity.[274]

As this chapter will demonstrate, Spurgeon agreed with each of Wills' tenets. The state should not levy penalties for a person's thoughts, especially regarding a person's religious conscience. The government should leave the dissenting churches alone and allow them to govern themselves under the authority of Scripture. While precedents were set in previous monarchies and administrations of British history in providing freedom of religious conscience, Spurgeon's sermons show that this battle still needed to be fought. Spurgeon was firmly entrenched in the camp of the Nonconformists, i.e., the Dissenters—a name derived from the Dissenters' unwillingness to conform to the rule of the Anglican Church as

---

[273] Spurgeon, *Autobiography* 1:69.

[274] Wills, *Democratic Religion: Freedom, Authority, and Church Discipline in the Baptist South 1785–1900*, 87–88.

outlined in the Book of Common Prayer (BCP). Ernest W. Bacon observed, "The Nonconformists were a formidable religious force in the life of the nation…Their strength was in the middle and working classes, and in the large towns."[275]

Baptists, whether Particular or General Baptists from the time of the 1600s, may not have agreed on everything, but L. Russ Bush and Tom J. Nettles showed that these Baptists shared a strong affirmation of the full deity and humanity of Christ, even endorsing the orthodox Christological creeds of the church. Both taught His threefold office of "prophet, priest, and king."[276] Of note, "Both groups rejected infant baptism in favor of believer's baptism, and both were deeply involved in the fight for religious liberty, separation of church and state, and liberty of conscience"[277] These Baptistic convictions are encapsulated in the confession of faith of The Southern Baptist Convention (SBC), founded in 1845 (around Spurgeon's eleventh birthday), that adopted a tenet expressed and clarified over time, coming into its present form in the *Baptist Faith and Message (2000)*, which began, "God alone is Lord of the conscience, and He has left it free from the doctrines and commandments of men which are contrary to His Word or not contained in it. Church and state should be separate. The state owes to every church protection and full freedom in the pursuit of its spiritual ends."[278]

---

[275] Bacon, *Spurgeon: Heir of the Puritans*, 7.

[276] Bush and Nettles, *Baptists and the Bible: The Baptist doctrines of biblical inspiration and religious authority in historical perspective*, 49.

[277] Ibid., 49.

[278] "XVII: Religious Liberty," *Baptist Faith and Message* (2000)(Nashville: LifeWay Press, 2000). It continues, "In providing for such freedom no ecclesiastical group or denomination should be favored by the state more than others. Civil government being ordained of God, it is the duty of Christians to render loyal obedience thereto in all things not contrary to the revealed will of God. The church should not resort to the civil power to carry on its work. The gospel of Christ contemplates spiritual means alone for the pursuit of its ends. The state has no right to impose penalties for religious opinions of any kind. The state has no right to impose taxes for the support of any form of religion. A free church in a free state is the Christian ideal, and this implies the right of free and unhindered access to God on the part of all men, and the right to form and propagate opinions in the sphere of religion without interference by the civil power."

As this chapter examines and evaluates Spurgeon's sermons, one will see that Spurgeon's convictions about religious liberty parallel the Baptist work from the past, and that those who followed Spurgeon's path mostly agreed with him. Spurgeon helped believers in his day to navigate the terrain of religious liberty. The question arises, from whom was Spurgeon wanting religious freedom?

Religious Freedom from Whom?

Spurgeon believed that the marriage between the Established Church and the government was a problematic alliance that confused the culture and shipwrecked souls. For Spurgeon, however, the issue was not merely about belonging to a certain religious group. All Spurgeon cared about ultimately was where he could find Christ:

> I think that sectarianism anywhere is an evil thing, but let no man ruin his soul for the sake of being a sectarian. If I were the strictest Churchman, I would rather go to heaven through hearing the gospel preached by a Dissenter than I would be lost in order to remain a staunch member of the Established Church; and if I were a Dissenter, I would sooner go to hear the gospel fully preached in the Church of England, and find Christ there, than I would go and sit down in my own conventicle, and listen to a sort of semi-Unitarianism of modern thought. The first and chief thing for my soul's good is that I must have Christ; and, for my part, I care not where I find Christ. Whether it be in a barn or in a cathedral, he is the same Christ to me. I would meet him on the mountain's brow if he bade me go there, but I would also meet him on the surface of the lake if he said to me as he said to Peter, "Come." Anywhere with Jesus, all is well; but away from Jesus, all is ill. Let nobody, then, refuse to accept Jesus Christ because of sectarian bigotry.[279]

This quote from an 1886 sermon exemplified Spurgeon's strong convictions and determination to preach and work toward religious

---

[279] Spurgeon, "Why Men Reject Christ," *MTP* 42:2463 (1886)

freedom in the culture and spiritual freedom that Christ provides. The notion that one's salvation and right standing before God were attributed to anything other than Christ was an egregious error. Historian David Bebbington observed:

> Spurgeon himself looked at affairs in an entirely different light. He called for disestablishment, among other reasons, because he believed that churches, unshackled by state interference, should single-mindedly spread the gospel rather than propagate particular cultural standards. There was no need for the Church of England to elevate the values of the common people because their attitudes were fundamentally sound already.[280]

As addressed in Chapter Three, the mixture of the political and religious authority was the reality in Spurgeon's England and a source of contention for the Nonconformist movement with which Spurgeon identified. Spurgeon struggled mightily with the pervasive influence of the Church of England. Though the Church of England broke away from Rome in the initial difference resided in who served as head of the church—with the answer now being the reigning English monarch rather than the Pope. England and many other European nations subscribed to the *divine-right* theory, which is the belief that monarchs derived their authority from God, not from any earthly authority.

In 1603, King James I of England (also King James VI of Scotland)(1566–1625) penned his treatise outlining this theory from his understanding not only of the Holy Scripture but also monarchical history.[281] These monarchs exercised their authority over the state, as well as the church. As James I clearly stated,

> Kings therefore, as God's deputies, judges upon earth, sit in thrones, clad with long robes, not as laikes and simply *togati* (as inferior secular judges are) but as *mixta persona* ... being bound to make a reckoning to GOD for their subjects souls as well as their bodies. Not that they ought to usurp any point of the

---

[280] Bebbington, "Spurgeon and the Common Man," *Baptist Theology and Review*, Spring 1995, 64.

[281] *The Workes of the Most High and Mightie Prince, James.*

Priestly office, no more then the Priest should the King's, for their two offices were divided in Aaron's priesthood; but it is the King's office to oversee and compel the Church to do her office, to purge all abuses in her, and by his sword ... to procure her due reverence and obedience of all his temporal subjects.[282]

One must notice the glaring hypocrisy on behalf of the Anglican Church. Henry VIII sought religious liberty from the faraway Papal rule for a rule established closer to home, freedom to worship according to his convictions. Yet, being the beneficiaries of obtaining this freedom, the Established Church repeatedly failed to provide that same religious liberty to others in his own land. The *divine-right* theory of rule, allying religion and politics, began because a monarch sought an avenue to divorce his wife, clearly against Catholic dogma and, more fundamentally, Scriptural mandates.

This inauspicious beginning of the Anglican Church faced many tensions (their monarch seeking an unbiblical divorce, breaking away from the Roman Catholic Church, how to deal with those who failed to conform to the new church, etc.), tensions of which Spurgeon was aware. Spurgeon always saw the Romish connection between the Roman Catholic Church and the Church of England. In Dale Warren Smith's unpublished work "The Victorian Preacher's Malady: The Metaphorical Usage of Gout in the Life of Charles Haddon Spurgeon," he observed, "There is little doubt that Spurgeon saw the Catholic Church as the great compromiser who had diluted the gospel into ineffectiveness. The robes or vestments of the priests, the rituals of the church, and the images of the saints all served to cloud the gospel, bringing the true church to the very being of destruction."[283] Just as the English government sought religious liberty from the Roman Catholic Church (and thus melded church and crown), there arose periods in English history where some sought the same freedom that the Anglican Church sought.

---

[282] *Workes*, 611.

[283] Smith, *"The Victorian Preacher's Malady: The Metaphorical Usage of Gout in the Life of Charles Haddon Spurgeon,"* (2017).

Yet, these tensions and struggles set a trajectory that continued throughout British history.

Spurgeon looked back on these tensions and struggles and drew several encouraging lessons—here invoking Oliver Cromwell (1599–1658), ruling as Lord Protector from 1653 to 1658 after leading the armies of Parliament in the English Civil War, contributing to the defeat of King Charles I. Cromwell noted in a letter in 1654:

> Religion was not the thing at first contested for, but God brought it to that issue at last, and gave it to us by way of redundancy, and at last it proved to be that which was most dear to us. And wherein this consisted more than in obtaining that liberty from the tyranny of the bishops to all species of Protestants to worship God according to their own light and conscience?[284]

Biographer Charles Firth noted that the program Cromwell sought to establish in his rule consisted of three things: "Manhood suffrage, annual Parliaments, and complete religious liberty." [285] Yes, Spurgeon saw Cromwell as an advocate of religious freedom.

In an 1855 sermon on the topic of "Spiritual Liberty," Spurgeon preached from 2 Corinthians 3:17: "Where the Spirit of the Lord is, there is liberty" (KJV). The sermon title indicated that the liberty of which Spurgeon spoke was of a spiritual nature. Yet, he connected this liberty to an ability to search out Christ freely without the compulsion of anyone or anything else. Again, invoking the name of Cromwell, Spurgeon showed the connection between spiritual liberty and religious freedom:

> Under the hand of God, I say, the men of religion—men like the great and glorious Cromwell, who would have liberty of conscience, or die—men who, if they could not reach kings' hearts, because they were unsearchable in cunning, would strike kings low, rather than they would be slaves. We owe our liberty to men of religion, to men of the stern Puritanical school—men

---

[284] Firth, *Oliver Cromwell and the Rule of the Puritans in England*, 52.
[285] Firth, *Cromwell*.

who scorned to play the craven and yield their principles at the command of man. And if we ever are to maintain our liberty (as God grant we may) it shall be kept in England by religious liberty—by religion. This Bible is the Magna Charta of old Britain. Its truths, its doctrines have snapped our fetters, and they never can be riveted on again, whilst men, with God's Spirit in their hearts, go forth to speak its truths. In no other land, save where the Bible is unclasped—in no other realm, save where the gospel is preached, can you find liberty.[286]

Thirty years after Cromwell's death, the Toleration Act of 1689 promised provisionally that the religious liberty for which Cromwell sought had been established by law. Yet, the victory was not as sweet as many Dissenters had hoped.

With the passing of the Act of Toleration, Dissenters found themselves in a period where religious liberty was possible. Calvinistic (Particular) Baptists used this opportunity to provide an updated, more detailed statement of faith. Thus, the Second London Confession was adapted from the original 1677 London Baptist Confession, which was revised from the *Savoy Declaration* of 1658, which, in turn, was a revised edition of the *Westminster Confession* (1647).[287] Yet, the Toleration Act permitted dissenting churches to worship freely with some caveats that went against the trajectory of toleration.

First, each dissenting church had to register with the government. Second, the government required each dissenting church to proclaim certain oaths of allegiance to the monarchy, who served as the head of the church. Failure to do so would entail dire consequences. Third, Nonconformists were still denied political office or the ability to teach at universities. Lastly, certain groups could not take a seat in Parliament. The freedom acquired was sparse, keeping the leverage with the Anglican Church.

While this Act provided more religious liberties for Dissenters than previously held, the inclusion came with so many

---

[286] Spurgeon, "Spiritual Liberty," *MTP* 1:9 (1855).
[287] Oliver, *History of the English Calvinistic Baptists 1771–1892: From John Gill to C.H. Spurgeon*, xvii-xviii.

caveats that the notion of "toleration" was infuriating to Nonconformists. One of Spurgeon's biographers, H.L. Wayland, captured the emotion of this arrangement:

> It is nothing to the purpose to say that there are among the clergy thus sustained by the State many polished gentlemen, many erudite scholars, many devout Christians. And it is liable to arouse emotions inconsistent with gospel meekness when the dignitaries in State and Church, after shutting out through generations and centuries the Nonconformists from the great universities and from social amenities and from the smiles of the court, then say, "You are not educated; you are not cultivated; you are not gentlemen."[288]

Spurgeon echoed Wayland along with other Dissenters who did not embrace the condescension dispensed by the Established Church of England in their use of the word "toleration":

> We are told that we enjoy *toleration*, the very word is an insult. What would the members of the dominant sect think if we talked of tolerating them? We shall never be satisfied until all religious communities stand upon an equal footing before the law. Cæsar has no right to demand of us that we shall support the religion or the superstition which he chooses to select. An Established Church is a spiritual tyranny. We wear no chains upon our wrists, but on our spirits our oppressors have thrust fetters which gall us worse than bands of steel. We are compelled as a part of the nation to support a church whose business it is to pull down that which with prayers and tears we live to build up, and would even die to maintain.[289]

Spurgeon saw through their diplomatic attempt—toleration was a condescending term that undermined the very notion they sought to convey. Yet, what did Spurgeon mean by "we are compelled to support?"

---

[288] Wayland, *Charles H. Spurgeon: His Faith and Works*, 207.

[289] Wayland, *Spurgeon*, 207.

In the same interview from the periodical *The Weekly Dispatch*, W.T. Stead interviewed Spurgeon at length in 1879, and inevitably the subject of the Established Church arose. While one may suppose that Spurgeon would mellow with age (by this time he was 45 years old), this particular subject left him as animated as ever. In the article entitled, "Eminent Radicals out of Parliament," Spurgeon had this to say,

> We wish success to those who advocate justice in religious liberty, be they who they may; but the important matter to us is the spiritual question, which must be kept apart ... the spiritual and political will not mix; in these days, at any rate....We will not by this question be brought into a parent union with those from whom we differ in the very core of our souls upon matters vital to Christianity.[290]

As mentioned in Chapter Three, Spurgeon believed in the potential good of the political process. He desired to see Christian men elected to lead a Christian nation. Yet, the joining of church and state into one authority over the citizens of England was something he did not desire.

The government compelled English citizens to support the Anglican Church monetarily, regardless of their religious conscience—much to the chagrin of Spurgeon, who through his preaching would mobilize those who advocated freedom of conscience. "Lovers of Religious Equality, your course is plain, and you will not leave your duty undone. With hand and heart support the men who would ride Religion of State Patronage and Control."[291] This patronage violated the consciences of believers like Spurgeon, showing that true equality did not exist. Given that most of those identifying as Dissenters (as mentioned earlier) were usually the poor or lower middle class of the citizenry, this required contribution caused more struggle for their own people—even as the

---

[290] Stead, "Eminent Radicals out of Parliament," *The Weekly Dispatch*, No. 5, November 9. 1879.

[291] Stead, "Eminent Radicals."

membership and attendance of the Anglican Church decreased during this time in English history.

Lest any readers of Stead's interview misunderstood Spurgeon's stance on the matter, he unequivocally leaned in,

> We can never rest until the Episcopacy is established and perfect religious equality is found everywhere. Leave to bury our dead in the graveyards which belong to every Englishman will be a liberty for which we will not even say 'thank you,' for it is no more than our right. As for the idea that this is the end of our demands, it is preposterous. There must be no patronage or oppression of any faith by the State, and all men must stand equal before the law whatever their creed may be; and until this is the case our demands will not cease.[292]

Spurgeon did not mince words. The "toleration" that the Church of England allowed Nonconformist churches to have was not theirs to give. Why say, "Thank you?" for what should serve as the baseline for liberty in the culture and the churches?

Spurgeon's Issue with the
Book of Common Prayer

The nomenclature of Spurgeon's ecclesiastical identification is that of Nonconformist, of whom he identified without reservation or apology. He held his Nonconformist views in perspective: "Conformity, or non-conformity, per se, is nothing; but a new creature is everything, and the truth upon which alone that new creature can live is worth dying a thousand deaths to conserve."[293] In another place, Spurgeon preached, "Great as civil or religious liberty may be, the liberty of my text transcendently exceeds. There is a liberty, dear friends, which Christian men alone enjoy; for even in Great Britain there are men who taste not the sweet air of

---

[292] Stead, "Eminent Radicals."

[293] Spurgeon, "Another Word concerning the Down Grade," *The Sword and the Trowel* 23:399 (1887). Quoted in Wills, "The Ecclesiology of Charles H. Spurgeon," *Baptist History and Heritage*, Autumn 1999, 76.

liberty."[294] A person is not saved based on the groups he joins but on receiving the work of Christ on the cross, Spurgeon would say.

Spurgeon believed in the full authority of Scripture in life and ministry. In an 1855 sermon, Spurgeon preached, "Stand over this volume, and admire its authority. This is no common book."[295] Did Spurgeon preach this tongue-in-cheek about the BCP? Spurgeon believed that the rule of Christendom lay in a more authoritative text than in the BCP:

> Brethren, we should never have had the errors of Rome back again among us if the Book of Common Prayer had been from the first conformed to the word of God. There were temporizers abroad of old who gained a present peace for themselves by leaving to their descendants, a heritage of error. We need to return to the pure word of God. Conform the church to the Scriptures, and quicken her with God's Spirit, and she will resist the encroachments of error; but fetter her with compromises, and she will become captive to falsehood ere long.[296]

A quick perusal of the table of contents of the BCP shows how the scripting of the liturgies or worship services, holy days, prayers, and ordinances were administered. The BCP also went so far as to give instructions (rules, more like) on marriage, visiting the sick, funerals, "the thanksgiving of women after Child-bearing," along with other special occasions. These instructions were not styled as mere suggestions, as would, say, a Minister's Manual that provides suggestions for worship services, weddings, funerals, and such. Spurgeon saw the BCP as an anchor and a way to provide orderliness for those who, by conviction, were a part of the Church of England. But he also saw the BCP as a weapon against Nonconformists, who as a result would commence in "cutting off occasion from them that seek occasion of cavil or quarrel against the Liturgy of the Church."[297]

---

[294] Spurgeon, "Spiritual Liberty," *MTP* 1:9 (1855).

[295] Spurgeon, "The Bible," *MTP* 1:15 (1855).

[296] Spurgeon, "Signs of the Times, *MTP* 19:1135 (1873).

[297] "Preface," *The Book of Common Prayer, and Administration of the Sacraments, and other Rites and Ceremonies of the Church, According to the Use*

How Spurgeon struggled with the notion of the Anglican liturgy. In addressing Spurgeon's time of family worship, Peter J. Morden observed, "Prayers [of Spurgeon] were always extempore (indeed he had an aversion to liturgy of any kind, holding that the practice of reading prayers, whether in private or public, encouraged empty, 'formal' devotions.)" [298] Yes, Spurgeon held strong convictions on this matter. In his *Morning by Morning; or Daily Readings for the Family or the Closet*, he wrote in the preface:

> We have written no prayers, because we think that a prayer is good for nothing if it be not written on the heart by the Holy Spirit, and made to gush forth warm from the soul. We should as soon think of printing a form for our children to use in addressing their parents, as draw up a form to be offered to our Father who is in heaven. It has been said in defense of forms, "Better to go on crutches than not at all;" but it is our firm conviction that those who truly *go* in the sense of worshipping aright, might with a little effort, and an earnest cry to the Holy Spirit for assistance, go much better on their own proper legs than upon the cripple's wearisome aids. [299]

Spurgeon believed that the church's authority lay in none other than Scripture and that pastors have the freedom to lead their churches according to the Bible's mandates, all the while free to use various methodologies in executing these mandates:

> Thou book of vast authority! thou art a proclamation from the Emperor of Heaven; far be it from me to exercise my reason in contradicting thee. Reason, thy place is to stand and find out what this volume means, not to tell what this book ought to say.

---

of the Church of England, Together with the Psalter or Psalms of David, Pointed as they are to be sung or said in Churches (Cambridge: The Church of England, 1662), 3.

[298] Morden, "C.H. Spurgeon and prayer," Evangelical Quarterly 84:4 (2012), 324.

[299] Spurgeon, *Morning by Morning, or Daily Readings for the Family or the Closet*, vii.

Come thou, my reason, my intellect, sit thou down and listen, for these words are the words of God.[300]

Spurgeon would say that the BCP was a collection of man's "reason" being conveyed as an authority over the Church. Spurgeon took umbrage with a particular practice, that of the priesthood.

Spurgeon's Issue with the Anglican Priesthood

According to the order of the BCP, the priesthood played a key role in the rites of the Anglican Church. Though Christ serves as the Church's Great High Priest (Hebrews 4:14), the Anglican Church would ordain *en masse* men to serve as priests to fulfill various aspects of church life. Christian George elaborates further:

Unlike Socinians who did not recognize Christ's priestly office, the Roman Catholics and Anglicans of nineteenth-century London produced their own priests in large quantities. Spurgeon allocated no small amount of ink to pointing out their theological blunders (for example, "The up-going of priests is the dishonour of the High Priest Christ Jesus)....For Spurgeon, the sacrifice for sin had already been offered; the path to reconciliation had already been paved. Any person who embraced the role of mediator was redundant, useless, and culpable of the severest of offences.[301]

To what "blunders" did Spurgeon refer? In a parenthetical remark in the above quote, George refers to an 1861 sermon in which Spurgeon noted, "The up-going of priests is the dishonour of the High Priest Christ Jesus; but when priestcraft ceases to be, and is cast down, then the Lord alone is exalted in that day."[302]

---

[300] Spurgeon, "The Bible."

[301] George, "An analysis of the doctrine of the priesthood of Jesus Christ in the functional Christology of Charles Haddon Spurgeon," *Theology in Scotland* (2011), 36.

[302] Spurgeon, "Temple Glories," *MTP* 7:375–78 (1861).

Spurgeon saw the practices of the Established Church as a residue of the Catholic Church, with the only difference lying in that it was headed by the presiding monarch of England rather than the Pope. Spurgeon saw the propitiation of sin already purchased and thus paved the way to the Father by the Son, the Church's Great High Priest. In an 1861 sermon, Spurgeon rebuffed the notion of the need of an earthly priesthood that exerted its influence over the people: "Our Lord Jesus Christ was ordained of God from of old, and did not of himself assume the position of high priest....Our Lord Jesus has been chosen, ordained, and glorified as our 'great high priest, that has passed into the heavens.' This is the ground-work of our comfort in our Lord Jesus."[303]

Yes, Spurgeon saw the role of these priests as redundant—men taking on the role that which only belongs to Christ. Spurgeon also saw this as a false practice of the church that enslaved the people into believing that absolution took place through any earthly institution:

Observe, according to the text, men have nothing to do with the selection; for here it is said, "I will also take of them"—not "their parents shall bring them up to it;" not "those who shall be looked out as the most fit and proper men on account of some natural bent and bias, or gift and talent, but I will take." God's priesthood in the world is a priesthood of his own choosing of his own setting apart, of his own anointing. "He hath made us kings and priests unto God." The church is a royal priesthood, not of man, neither by man, nor of the will of man, nor of blood, nor of birth: it is of God's choosing.[304]

Spurgeon preached how Christians may freely approach the throne of God, as all Christians are a royal priesthood. In a sermon based on 1 Peter 2:4–5, Spurgeon recognized that there were those "who condemn us because we reject the pomp of their ceremonial, the prestige of their state connection, and the venerableness of their

---

[303] Spurgeon, "Our Sympathizing High Priest," 32:1927 (1886).
[304] Spurgeon, "A New Order of Priests and Levites," 17:992 (1871).

antiquity."[305] Yet, Spurgeon saw the basis for their rejections, and always remembered what Christ intended for the priesthood:

> These have weight with the unlearned and unspiritual, but those who are taught of God discern the vanity of their boastings. Be not moved by their judgment, no, not for an hour, for if you indeed come to the Lord Jesus you are built up by himself into a spiritual house, and that which he doeth does not lack for honour or reverence.[306]

Spurgeon, The Great Commoner in England

Due to Spurgeon's status among the Nonconformists (the Metropolitan Tabernacle was the largest in England), he became the *de facto* leader among their religious tribe in breaking the shackles of their authoritarian rule. Again, biographer J.D. Hall shed light on Spurgeon's thinking:

> The Church of England—I mean the State Church—well-nigh overshadowed everything. Non-conformity lacked a great leader. There were but a few great preachers when Spurgeon appeared, but his pure Anglo-Saxon words, his terse idioms, his apt illustrations, his marvelous voice, his vein of humor, his common sense, his broad liberalism in politics—for Spurgeon was the great Commoner in England—all these helped him.[307]

"The Great Commoner in England." Hall recalled how Spurgeon's style of preaching differed greatly from the slick and scripted oratory coming from the pulpits of the Anglican churches. This mode of preaching that Spurgeon employed connected well with the vulnerable and downtrodden, and demonstrated that at least one church and one pastor cared for their souls, even though their

---

[305] Spurgeon, "The True Priesthood, Temple and Sacrifice," *MTP* 23:1376 (1877).

[306] Spurgeon, "The True Priesthood."

[307] Hall, "Spurgeon As I Knew Him." 138.

situation could offer little else materially. Spurgeon clearly saw not only the significance of reaching this stratum of society but the importance for everyone to have the freedom to worship as their conscience dictates—even to the point where a Christian has the freedom to worship as Christianly as conscience dictates.

Spurgeon's own demeanor and deportment in carrying out his ministry saw him obtain a definite connection to the vulnerable and downtrodden in society. Spurgeon saw the needs around him that the Established Church and the government failed to address. Although Spurgeon's attitudes toward the classics were ones of respect, he did not see the need to teach them to his congregation. Bebbington reflected on Spurgeon's contemporary, the "poet, literary critic and upholder of classical ideals, Matthew Arnold, who in J. Dover Wilson's edition of *Culture and Anarchy* wrote in 1869:

> Might it not, then, be urged with great force that the way to do good, in presence of this operation for uprooting the Church establishment in Ireland by the power of the Nonconformists' antipathy to publicly establishing or endowing religious worship, is not by lending a hand straight away to the operation, and Hebraizing,—that is, in this case, taking an uncritical interpretation of certain Bible words as our absolute rule of conduct,—with the Nonconformists. It may be very well for born Hebraizers, like Mr. Spurgeon, to Hebraize; but for Liberal statesmen to Hebraize is surely unsafe, and to see poor old Liberal hacks Hebraizing, whose real self belongs to a kind of negative Hellenism,—a state of moral indifferency without intellectual ardour,—is even painful. And when, by our Hebraizing, we neither do what the better mind of statesmen prompted them to do, nor win the affections of the people we want to conciliate, nor yet reduce the opposition of our adversaries but rather heighten it, surely it may be not unreasonable to Hellenize a little, to let our thought and consciousness play freely about our proposed operation and its motives, dissolve these motives if they are unsound, which certainly they have some appearance, at any rate, of being, and create in their stead, if they are, a set of sounder and more persuasive motives conducting to a more solid operation. May

not the man who promotes this be giving the best help towards finding some lasting truth to minister to the diseased spirit of his time, and does he really deserve that the believers in action should grow impatient with him?[308]

In other spots in Arnold's chapter, Bebbington reflected that Arnold saw Spurgeon as "a boor, a despiser of culture, a Hebraizer who showed an obsession with religion to the exclusion of the humane values of ancient Greece." [309] As this chapter will note later, Bebbington added to the number of witnesses who recognize that "like Luther, Spurgeon was quite content to court controversy" and in a "gesture of defiance, he erected a baptismal font in his garden as a bird bath."[310] Bebbington also noted that "Spurgeon flaunted a hearty John Bull style of patriotism that lauded his own country as a land of freedom."[311]

Horton Davies noted that Spurgeon's association with the Baptist denomination did him no favors regarding the established authorities of the day. When comparing the champion of the Baptist denomination with a champion of the Anglicans, George Whitefield (1714–1770), Davies contends that Spurgeon's association with his denomination was a struggle, numbering him with those who struggled in finding a station in the upper strata of society:

Spurgeon was a better organizer of institutions and of sermons than Whitefield. Spurgeon had to overcome the disadvantage of being a Dissenter minister in England, where every Anglican clergyman enjoys some degree of social prestige; Whitefield was an Anglican, and he succeeded equally well with the rich and the poor, the aristocrats and the paupers. Spurgeon's success was chiefly with the lower middle-classes and artisans.[312]

---

[308] Arnold, *Culture and Anarchy,* J. Dover Wilson, ed., 210–11.

[309] Bebbington, *The Dominance of Evangelicalism: The Age of Spurgeon to* Moody, 42

[310] Bebbington, *Evangelicalism,* 42.

[311] Bebbington, *Evangelicalism,* 43.

[312] Davies, "Expository Preaching: Charles Haddon Spurgeon," *Foundations* 6 (1963) 18.

Whitefield contended the Anglicans succeeded "equally well with the rich and poor, the aristocrats and the paupers" while Spurgeon could only interact with and connect with the lower classes due to his lack of "social prestige" from being outside the Anglican fold. While this designation by Whitefield (and others who identified with the Established Church) may have insulted some, Spurgeon may have seen this as a badge of honor. The belief by the Anglican Church of its superiority over all other Christian beliefs outside the Established Church's fold is demonstrated in Whitefield's remarks—and helps one comprehend Spurgeon's connection with the vulnerable of his day and why; truth be told, he did not value impressing the elite of society to obtain a celebrity's edge. He cultivated an authentic style, which was easily understood among the masses as a by-product. At the same time, Spurgeon suffered for his stance as a Dissenting Baptist. The quote from Whitefield also betrays the underlying view many had of Spurgeon's countenance, preaching style, and stances on matters such as religious liberty.

All Religions on Equal Footing

Spurgeon sought to have all religions on equal footing. The sermon that most outlined Spurgeon's belief in the freedom of conscience and religious liberty was his 1861 sermon delivered at the Metropolitan Tabernacle by Henry Vincent called, "Nonconformity." Henry Vincent, best known for his book, *The Story of the Commonweal: The Complete and Graphic Narrative of the Origin and Growth of the Movement* (that is, the industrial movement), stood as an advocate for suffrage movements for women and workers, as well as Dissenters against the authority of the Anglican Church.[313] A gifted orator and historian, Vincent outlined the history of England and told the story of those following their religious conscience even at the expense of the wrath of the monarchy. Even back to the reign of James I in the 1520s, Vincent recalled,

---

[313] Vincent, *The Story of the Commonweal: The Complete and Graphic Narrative of the Origin and Growth of the Movement*, xiii.

But, blessed be God, this may be the language of time-servers, but it is not the language of the Gospel of Jesus Christ, and the Church produced men and women who confronted the powers of darkness and oppression in vindication of the gospel; and will you tell me that that cloud of women and men who went to the stake in the county of Kent, in the county of Essex, in this great metropolis, that holy band of men and women who went to the stake at Gloucester, at Oxford, at Coventry, at Derby—from one end of England to the other, numbering upwards of four hundred persons, many of them beneficed clergymen—and will you tell me that they died for Episcopacy? No, they died for the Gospel, and they were Nonconformists! When they died, they refused to conform to the established order of things; and mind you, I do not want to flatter dissent. There have been as many good Nonconformists in the Church as out of it, and you have found that those Nonconformists in the Church, and then the Nonconformists out of the Church have saved religion and liberty, and have been the glory of the country in which we have the happiness to dwell."[314]

Vincent's argument lay in history's rendering of the true nature of British law and historical record that religious freedom was intended as a reality centuries ago, removing the need for Parliament to (intentionally or otherwise) serve as an "oppressive body" to its own conscience-driven citizens.[315]

---

[314] Vincent, "Nonconformity," *MTP* 7:399 (1861).

[315] Vincent, "Nonconformity," "...that the laws of England are intended to protect all men in the honest exercise of their religious opinions. The scholars, taking this ground on scholarship alone, attracted the attention of the more earnest Christians, and these earnest Christians said, 'These scholars speak wisely, for the Scriptures of truth give to us the right to worship God according to the dictates of our own conscience;" so that under the current there welled up—partly from the Universities, partly from the Lords and Commons, partly from the Presbyterian and Dissenting Meeting-houses, partly from the Nonconforming body in the Church—there welled up these grand ideas, that the Parliament of England, consisting of Crown, Lords, and Commons, ought not to be an oppressive body, and that every man who was loyal to the crown, and obeyed the laws, ought to enjoy perfect liberty with every other man in the kingdom."

Spurgeon struggled with the "unholy alliances" that church and government made with one another. For many churches and their pastors, the temptation in obtaining "state endowments and grants" was difficult to resist. In an 1855 sermon, Spurgeon made his convictions clear,

> [Those] who stand out for the royal supremacy of the Saviour, and look only to Christ as the head of the Church. They apply to us the epithets of "schismatics," "dissenters," and such-like, but I believe that God shall yet say of every state-church, whether it be the Church of England, Ireland, Scotland or of anywhere else, "Go ye up upon her walls, and destroy; but make not a full end;" for there are thousands of pious men in her midst, 'take away her battlements; for they are not the Lord's.'"[316]

The Anglican Church's problematic connection with the government would play itself out at various points in British history. The Irish Famine of 1845, both its background regarding the relationship between the Anglicans and the Irish Catholics and the famine itself, stands as a concrete example of the absence of religious liberty.

The Reaction to the Irish Famine of 1845

Spurgeon again showed his remarkable grasp of English history in an 1859 sermon, where he alluded to the heartaches of the Irish Famine of 1845.

> We have heard of a famine in Ireland, and some dreadful stories have been related to us that have harrowed our hearts and almost made our hair stand up on end; but even there the full fury of famine was not known. We have heard too, to our great grief, that there are still in this city, dark and hideous spots, where men and women are absolutely perishing from hunger, who have sold

---

[316] Spurgeon, "Storming the Battlements," *MTP* 1:38 (1855).

from off their backs the last rags that covered them, and are now unable to leave the house, and positively perishing of famine.[317]

This tragic season in Irish history magnifies one sad commentary on how the dominance of the Church of England and its alliance with the monarchy occurred to the detriment of the Irish people. The history between the British and the Irish was a long and contentious one. Susan Campbell Bartoletti, author of *Black Potatoes: The Story of the Great Irish Famine, 1845–1850*, conveys how the Catholic Irish fought against the British in their effort to colonize Ireland but in 1690 were defeated by King William of Orange (a Protestant). Soon, Parliament acted to bring forth a set of laws known as the Penal Laws to keep the Irish Catholics in their submissive place.

Under the Penal Laws, Catholics were forbidden to vote, hold political office, carry or own firearms, engage in certain trades or professions, or provide their children with a Catholic education. They could not purchase land or bequeath their land as they wished. They were also forbidden to possess a horse worth more than five pounds.[318]

Approximately one hundred years later, British Prime Minister William Pitt sought to bring England, Scotland, Wales, and Ireland into the United Kingdom with the Act of Union. Irish Catholics believed this would bring them to equal terms under the law. They could send representatives to Parliament and could participate in the largest economy in the world. Again, Bartoletti provides understanding:

Ireland was allowed to elect only a small number of representatives to Parliament, which gave them little legislative power. Irish Catholics had hoped to have their political rights restored, but this did not happen. Only Members of the wealthy Protestant landlord class were eligible to take a seat in

---

[317] Spurgeon, "Corn in Egypt," *MTP* 5:234 (1859).

[318] Bartoletti, *Black Potatoes: The Story of the Great Irish Famine, 1845–1850*, Kindle location 144.

Parliament. This left Catholics, laborers, farmers, businessmen, and women without a vote.[319]

This gives some background to Britain's lack of religious liberty to other nations under the umbrella of the United Kingdom. A mere sixteen years after the passing of the Catholic Emancipation Act, Ireland's eight million population (the densest country in Europe) suffered a famine that threatened its mere existence of this country. Of those eight million, three million lived in poverty and squalid conditions.

When the famine took over, many Irish families faced a choice: Try to survive or leave with an aim for a better life. As mentioned in Chapter Two, two million left Ireland, many going to America or Canada—yet approximately 600,000 went to England. The British government struggled with how to approach this influx of Irish (especially the Irish Catholics) who crossed the English borders. This sad trajectory of the British government toward their fellow UK citizens due to their race and even more so their religion serves as a concrete example of how religious liberty existed for certain groups of people, but not for everyone.

Freedom of Conscience
Affects the Entire Nation

Spurgeon noted how religious liberty affected the liberty not merely of the religious organizations themselves but the entire nation. As stated previously, like other Baptists, he believed in religious liberty for all—liberty to follow one's conscience so long as one's conscience does not infringe on the rights or harm another. Spurgeon was a spiritual descendant from the Colonial Baptists in the New World who faced religious persecution. The following example shows: (1) how Spurgeon's connections with the Baptists were nothing new, even in a land seeking religious liberty from the Anglican Church; and (2) that as religious liberty was sought in

---

[319] Bartoletti, *Black Potatoes,* Kindle location 165. In 1829, the Catholic Emancipation Act was passed, but this did not assuage the anger toward the "British rule and English landlordism."

Colonial America, so too did Spurgeon seek religious liberty in England.

Colonial America
Paralleling British History

Another instance of the Anglican Church's tension in permitting religious freedom for British citizens happened in one of their colonies—the American colonies. For Americans early on, historian Stephen Prothero of Boston University observes in his work, *Why Liberals Win the Culture Wars (Even When They Lose Elections)* how many of the issues that have transpired in the political realm over American history often dealt with "the two bedrock principles of American life ... religious liberty and private property."[320] Yet, the history of America has demonstrated a struggle to define what religious liberty means in light of the Established Church's shadow. While the scope of this chapter is not about America's present struggle, America began as a colony of England in a desire to worship Christ freely by the dictates of their own conscience.

At the beginning of the American experiment, men such as Baptist pastor John Leland (1754–1841) fought for religious liberty in the American colonies:

The plea for religious liberty has been long and powerful; but it has been left for the United States to acknowledge it a right inherent, and not a favor granted: to exclude religious opinions from the list of objects of legislation. Sunday schools and missionary societies are of long standing; but camp-meetings and protracted meetings (in their present mode of operation) are novel. What changes may hereafter take place, to me is uncertain. None, however, that will change the character of God, destroy the reach of tyrants.[321]

---

[320] Prothero, *Why Liberals Win the Culture Wars (Even When They Lose Elections): The Battles That Define America from Jefferson's Heresies to Gay Marriage*, 20.

[321] Leland, *The Writings of the Late Elder John Leland, Including Some Events in His Life*, 31.

Regarding religious liberty, Leland had an influential relationship with soon-to-be Founding Fathers James Madison and Thomas Jefferson and was deemed an "ally" among numerous other political leaders by Jefferson until Leland's death in 1841.[322] As a result, colonial Baptists developed an interesting alliance with Thomas Jefferson during the 1800 presidential election, as the presidential candidate was by no means an evangelical Christian but was still someone who saw the value of religious liberty. For Jefferson, seeking independence from Great Britain meant seeking independence from the Church with whom the government was aligned. Baptists, influenced by Leland, found an ally for religious liberty in an unlikely source, but it was not always so in colonial times. Spurgeon noted the hypocrisy of the Anglican Church that began with a desire for religious liberty yet failed to provide that for those outside the Anglican Church. That same hypocrisy occurred in colonial Virginia.

Baptists were under persecution from the British government at the beginning of the American Revolution. Thomas Kidd and Barry Hankins observed, "As Virginia moved toward establishing a state government independent from Britain, Baptists continued to petition for full religious liberty. Again, they implied that refusing to afford liberty of conscience would encourage divisions among Virginians when unity was needed most."[323] Virginia Baptists struggled with the notion of fighting alongside their fellow colonists who, on the one hand, sought freedom from the British and the Establishment Church while, on the other hand, refused to allow them the freedom to worship according to their consciences.

One Virginian, James Madison, at merely twenty-three-years old, saw the persecution Baptists endured in his colony and worked to broaden the intent of the language in the tenet of "freedom of religion." John Leland and Madison worked diligently on this project. As such, his work was codified in the Virginia Declaration

---

[322] Scarberry, "John Leland and James Madison: Religious Influence on the Ratification of the Constitution and on the Proposal of the Bill of Rights," *Penn State Law Review* 113:3 (2009), 738–39.

[323] Kidd and Hankins, *Baptists in America: A History*, 63.

of Rights, written by George Mason, and adopted by the Virginia Constitutional Convention of 1776. This document affirmed,

> That religion, or the duty to which we owe to our Creator, and the manner of discharging it, can be directed only by reason and conviction, not by force or violence; and therefore all men are equally entitled to the free exercise of religion, according to the dictates of conscience, and that it is the mutual duty of all to practice Christian forbearance, love, and charity towards each other.[324]

As expressed previously, the hypocrisy that existed in England existed in colonial America: The trajectory of their respective countries began with an aim for religious liberty (the Anglican Church with England, colonial America across the Atlantic) but then turned around and denied that same liberty to others. On both sides of the Atlantic, Baptists suffered persecution by being denied religious liberty—and thus became (as Gregory Wills noted previously) champions of freedom of conscience to worship. In 1857, Spurgeon continued to remind church and culture alike of the benefits that come with religious liberty standing as an unmovable conviction:

> Religion must be the foundation of every blessing which society can hope to enjoy. Little as men think it, religion has much to do with our liberty, our happiness, and our comfort. England would not have been what it now is, if it had not been for her religion; and in that hour when she shall forsake her God, her glory shall have fallen, and 'Ichabod' shall be written upon her banners.[325]

Spurgeon's life would have been under threat should he have decided to come to America. "The boycott was effective in that it had a devastating effect on Spurgeon. He experienced a great amount of stress and anguish over the financial hardship that it

---

[324] Article XVI of the Virginia Declaration of Rights, George Mason's Draft, and Final Version, in Dreisach and Hall, *Sacred Rights of Conscience*, 241.
[325] Spurgeon, "The War of Truth," *MTP* 3:112 (1857).

placed on his ministry."[326] The financial difficulties due to a boycott of his sermons hurt other projects in which he endeavored—much to Spurgeon's consternation. Religious liberty entails the freedom to worship and the freedom to comment about the actions of the government and even dissent—but not freedom for all actions.

A Nation with Religious Liberty is More Receptive to the Gospel

From a spiritual vantage point, Spurgeon saw the benefit of religious liberty in the English culture. When religious liberty is a cultural reality, the opportunity for the gospel to spread is possible. As mentioned previously, Spurgeon's view of religious liberty and freedom of conscience did not mean that he saw each religion as inherently equal in achieving the same salvific ends. The freedom to pursue one's religious beliefs is done so because of a principle that these convictions are not only correct, but that freedom should exist to demonstrate their correctness to others. As such, Spurgeon believed that religious liberty allowed a nation to be more receptive to (among other faith systems) the gospel of Christ—and that Christians should take advantage of this capability for the glory of God and the good of all other respective cultures:

> Let the Christian element spread, and it will be a power to bless mankind. It shall, in proportion as it spreads, put down evil, and foster good. Already, many a monopoly has been ended, and many a liberty has been gained. Much religious intolerance has been subdued by the power of Jesus Christ over his people; and I do pray, dear friends, that we may live to see all nations more manifestly affected by the gospel of Jesus Christ. May every nation be ruled by just and righteous laws! May every nation be willing to submit exterior disputes to the arbitration of justice! It

---

[326] Rose, "Spurgeon and the Slavery Controversy of 1860: A Critical Analysis of the Anthropology of Charles Haddon Spurgeon, as it relates specifically to his Stance on Slavery," *Midwestern Journal of Theology* 16:1 (2017), 28.

will be so one day. The nations shall be friends, and all men shall feel that they are members of one great family.[327]

Spurgeon's convictions as outlined in the above quote are telling. First, Spurgeon believed that Christianity had the "power to bless mankind" by putting down evil and perpetuating good. Secondly, Spurgeon believed Christianity provided liberty and subdued religious intolerance. Lastly, Spurgeon proclaimed how Christianity dispensed just laws. While Spurgeon operated from a biblical worldview and could be accused of holding bias toward Christianity, he believed that enough evidence existed from Scripture and history to demonstrate the validity of these convictions.

Even though Spurgeon detested the alliance of church and government, he found hope that some in the Church of England sought to sever those alliances in a search for freedom from the government's influence:

Even now we see a stir throughout the world to take away these battlements. The holy and pious men in the Church of England have multiplied amazingly during the last few years. It is pleasing to see the great improvement in the Establishment. I think no class of Christians have made more speedy advances in reformation than they have. They have a stirring in their midst, and are saying, 'Why should we be under the government any longer?' There are many clergymen who have said, 'We have no wish whatever for this union: we would be glad to come away from all state control.' I wonder they do not do it, and follow their convictions.[328]

Spurgeon held out hope that those in the Church of England who desired removal of the marriage between church and state would "follow their convictions." Yes, Spurgeon hoped for another reformation—this time in the Church of England.

As this chapter moves to construct Spurgeon's ethic regarding religious liberty, one should interact with this quote from

---

[327] Spurgeon, "Jesus: All Blessing and All Blest," *MTP* 37:2187 (1891).
[328] Spurgeon, "Storming the Battlements."

an 1864 sermon. Spurgeon saw the sovereignty of God at work in his beloved England where the gospel was sent and preached, while other nations did not yet have such privileges. Yet, Spurgeon hoped that God would move to bring the gospel to these lands where these citizens would experience the freedom of Christ and, one would also pray, the freedom to worship Christ according to their conscience:

> Yet to us the gospel is graciously sent, so that few nations enjoy it so fully as we do. It is true that Prussia and Holland hear the Word, and that Sweden and Denmark are comforted by the truth, but their candle burns but dimly; it is a poor flickering lamp which cheers their darkness, while in our own dear land, partly from the fact of our religious liberty, and yet more graciously through the late revival, the sun of the gospel shines brightly, and men rejoice in the light of day. Why this? Why no grace for the Japanese? Why no gospel preached to the inhabitants of Central Africa? Why was not the truth of God displayed in the Cathedral of Santiago, instead of the mummeries and follies which disgraced both dupes and deceivers, and were the incidental cause of the horrible burnings of that modern Tophet? Why to-day is not Rome, instead of being the seat of the beast, become the throne of Jesus Christ? I cannot tell you. But assuredly, divine sovereignty passing by many races of men, has been pleased to pitch upon the Anglo-Saxon family, that they may be as the Jews were aforetime, the custodians of divine truth, and the favorites of mighty grace.[329]

Spurgeon wished for religious liberty to exist throughout the world, which would open the doors for others to come in and know about the sufficiency of Christ in all things.

---

[329] Spurgeon, "Election No Discouragement to Seeking Souls," *MTP* 10:553 (1864).

Effects of Spurgeon's Fight
as a Dissenting Baptist

As this chapter examined Spurgeon's views of religious liberty from the standpoint of a Dissenting Baptist, he would warn those in the pew and classroom of the effects of fighting for such a noble cause and the controversies that are bound to ensue. Spurgeon observed to his students at the Pastors' College: "To win a soul from going down into the pit is a more glorious achievement than to be crowned in the arena of theological controversy as *Doctor Sufficientissimus....* [Be] prepared to fight, and always have your sword buckled on your thigh, but wear a scabbard."[330] Yet, Spurgeon's fight came at a significant cost relationally, emotionally, and ministerially. These fights were "deeply personal" and as such would affect him physically as well.[331]

While Spurgeon fought for the freedom of an individual believer to pursue his beliefs according to their own conscience, those within his own denomination took that message to heart and moved in their own personal direction, that which was away from orthodoxy. As a result, Spurgeon's long-standing fight with those in the Established Church all but ceased due to his concern of the direction of his Baptist association. In referencing Spurgeon changing his confrontation with the established church, Hopkins observed,

There was a catholic streak in Spurgeon that helped nurture this respect; this developed most in his last years when he more or less broke off hostilities on the Catholic front to concentrate his firepower on what he considered the more serious and dangerous

---

[330] Spurgeon, *Lectures to My Students, 4 volumes in one* (Pasadena, TX: Pilgrim Publications, 1990), 1:83, 2:43f. Quoted in Tom Nettles, *Living by Revealed Truth: The Life and Pastoral Theology of Charles Haddon Spurgeon* (Ross-shire, Scotland: Christian Focus Publications, 2013), 471.

[331] Morden, *Communion with Christ and His People: The Spirituality of C.H. Spurgeon*, 104.

errors of liberalism. He had long recognized spirituality in the High Church when he had come into contact with it.[332]

Tom Nettles noted,

> When one critic suggested that Spurgeon's accusations came from sickness, not his theological acumen, he showed his entire disgust with this dodging of theological issues....His solemn observations about theology are suggested by his pain, according to the critic, not his brain. This lack of Christian courtesy showed, in Spurgeon's judgment, that the new theology had introduced a new tone and spirit.[333]

Nettles reflected on another historian of English Baptists, A.C. Underwood, who unfairly insulted Spurgeon's intellect. Nettles commented on Underwood's remarks, "Underwood has added to the insult by implying that Spurgeon was simply intellectually incapable of appreciating the advances of modern thought." Underwood called him, "A sick man, he viewed with deepest concern all departure from the theology of the Puritans."[334] Clearly, Spurgeon's teachings on religious liberty, especially from his Baptist background, would bring along many more insults before his day was done.

One of Spurgeon's students and biographer J.C. Carlile observed regarding the Downgrade Controversy,

> Spurgeon had nothing to gain by entering into the controversy. He was a sick man suffering agonies of pain; indeed, he was marked for death. He had a great and unsullied reputation, with friends and admirers in both camps. Nothing less than an overwhelming conception of duty to the faith he proclaimed and the Lord he honoured could have sent him into the arena.[335]

---

[332] Hopkins, *Nonconformity's Romantic Generation: Evangelical and Liberal Theologies in Victorian England* (Wipf and Stock Publishers, 2007), 160.

[333] Nettles, 630.

[334] Underwood, *A History of the English Baptists*, 231. Quoted Nettles, 630.

[335] Carlile, *Charles H. Spurgeon*, 243.

Churches pressured Spurgeon to stand up to the new modernistic theology that crept in. He would fight, yes, but Carlisle continued, "He hated controversy and obviously was not a skillful [*sic*] controversialist."[336]

Many of the key doctrines that Spurgeon taught from the Scriptures—doctrines that Baptists long held—were discarded as the effects of Darwinism (Chapter Four) and the higher critical method began to gain credence. The spiritual effects of the revival that had taken place just two decades earlier were waning. Willis Glover noted that, in hindsight, Spurgeon's concerns about the wavering of the church's theological moorings were "apprehensions … not without foundation…This emphasis, Spurgeon saw, was being lost, and he saw the cause in the wavering uncertainty produced by theological laxity."[337]

Spurgeon recognized that the Baptist Union did not have the constitutional power to hold any of the churches to a doctrinal system. Spurgeon would exert his freedom of conscience, withdraw from the Baptist Union and focus on pastoring the Metropolitan Tabernacle. As Joel Gregory put it: "The deed was done. The largest controversy in British Baptist history would run from October 28, 1887, to the meeting of the Union in London at City Temple on April 23, 1888, where James Archer Spurgeon, brother of the preacher, not only seconded a compromise motion but also stayed in the Union."[338]

The loss of relationships and brotherly fellowship would emotionally fracture Spurgeon until his death less than four years later. Biographer Golden Pike echoed the sadness of Spurgeon's heart,

Mr. Spurgeon's last years were, to some extent, embittered by sorrows to which he had been a stranger in earlier days. There can be no doubt that what will be known in history as the Down-grade Controversy threw a chilling shadow over this great and

---

[336] Carlile, *Spurgeon*, 243–44.

[337] Glover, "English Baptists at the Time of the Downgrade Controversy," *Foundations*, 47.

[338] Gregory, "Spurgeon's Resignation from the British Baptist Union: A Microhistory of First Responders," *Baptist History & Heritage*, Fall 2018, 35.

good man's life, causing him pain or sorrow of heart which could not but have a more or less disastrous influence on his health.[339]

Conclusion

The next chapter of this work is the concluding chapter which constructs the gospel-centered ethic toward the vulnerable regarding patriotism, nationalism, racism, and religious liberty.

---

[339] Pike, *Charles Haddon Spurgeon* (London: Cassell and Company Limited, 1893), 112.

Conclusion

The thesis for this work, as stated in Chapter One, constructs a set of principles for evangelical Christians to use in ministering to and caring for the vulnerable and downtrodden in their society and the world to fulfill Christ's command to love one's neighbor. This set of principles has its basis in searching and analyzing the sermons of Charles Spurgeon. This systematic examination of Spurgeon's sermons led to the construction of an ethic toward the vulnerable and downtrodden. Even now, almost 130 years after Spurgeon's death, the evangelical world (and the non-evangelical world, for that matter) still needs the words of Spurgeon to help the contemporary church contemplate and work through their modern-day issues.

This concluding chapter constructs an ethic that addresses the issue of patriotism/nationalism, racism, and religious liberty. This chapter culls from the respective chapters of this work the ethical principles that Spurgeon tackled in his preaching. Next, this chapter shows how each of these areas connects to the thesis. Finally, this chapter demonstrates five insights for a gospel-centered ministry toward the vulnerable based on Spurgeon's preaching and work.

Summarizing Chapter One:
Introduction

Chapter One introduced the thesis of this work to provide a gospel-centered ethic toward the vulnerable from an examination of Spurgeon's sermons. This chapter provided a brief biography of Spurgeon's ministry and, specifically, how his ministry connected to those considered vulnerable by society. Spurgeon's entry onto the London scene at the age of nineteen opened his eyes to the vulnerable who lined the streets and filled the houses throughout London. From nineteen-years-old until he died at the age of fifty-seven, Spurgeon continued to preach the Scriptures and use the Word to perpetually advocate for those less fortunate members of society.

Chapter One also addressed the personal vulnerabilities of Spurgeon, from his mental to his physical health, which aided him in his empathy toward others who also endured daily struggles. The criticisms he experienced at the expense of the press early on in his ministry, and the fractured relationship between his denomination and himself toward the end, affected every aspect of his health and well-being. The loss of friendships also played a part in exacerbating his suffering.

Spurgeon's theology was formative in the creation of his ethic. His embracing of the teaching that all humans are made in the image of God (Gen 1:27–28) laid the groundwork for God's lack of partiality among the peoples of the nations and the second part of the Great Commandment: "Love your neighbor as yourself." Spurgeon's belief in the doctrine of substitutionary atonement extended to the poor and weak among them. This chapter also included personal anecdotes from his sermons to show that Spurgeon did not simply preach about ministering to the vulnerable—he ministered actively among them.

Chapter One connected to the thesis by laying a foundation for the need to construct an ethic toward the vulnerable, not simply to add to Spurgeon scholarship, but to be of use to the church of Jesus Christ in every generation.

Summarizing Chapter Two:
Interacting with Spurgeon Scholarship

Chapter Two examined significant works that address Spurgeon's aim and desire to engage with the vulnerable and downtrodden in society through the preaching of the gospel. This chapter examined several biographies of Spurgeon and works about his struggles, pastoral ministry, and theological convictions. While many authors have addressed the various stages and issues of Spurgeon's life and ministry before, this work was needed to understand his ethic specifically toward the vulnerable during his time to help evangelicals do the same in the present.

In connecting with the thesis, Chapter Two showed the need for works that address issues of patriotism/nationalism, racism, and religious liberty from Spurgeon's preaching, demonstrating how Christianity seeks to push back against these atrocities. With the prevalence of conversation taking place in all strata of government and churches, markedly absent in the overall corpus of Spurgeon scholarship are works that discuss these topics specifically. The goal is to develop a gospel-centered ethic toward the vulnerable, adding to the overall literature dedicated to Spurgeon's life and ministry.

Summarizing Chapter Three:
Nationalism and Imperialism in Great Britain

Chapter Three examined Spurgeon's preaching regarding the patriotism/nationalism/imperialism of Great Britain. First, Spurgeon believed that heavenly citizenship served as a Christian's primary citizenship. When addressing matters of nationalism and patriotism, Christians must continually remember the foundation of how they live in their country of citizenship. Even as Christians treasure the citizenship of their country, if they allow that allegiance to usurp their devotion to Christ, they must repent. In an 1860 sermon, Spurgeon spoke about an old legend that celebrated the patriotism of Rome's bravest. With this, he connected this legend to what Christ asks of his church:

> Or, read you that old legend of Curtius, the Roman knight. A great gulf had opened in the Forum, perhaps caused by an earthquake, and the auspices had said that the chasm could never be filled up, except the most precious thing in Rome could be cast into it. Curtius puts on his helmet, and his armour, mounts his horse and leaps into the cleft, which is said to have filled at once, because courage, valour, and patriotism, were the best things in Rome. I wonder how many Christians there are who would leap like that into the cleft. Why, I see you, sirs, if there is a new and perilous work to be done for Christ, you like to be in the rear rank this time; if there were something honourable,

so that you might ride on with your well caparisoned steeds in the midst of the dainty ranks ye would do it; but to leap into certain annihilation for Christ's sake—Oh! heroism, where is it fled—whither has it gone. Thou Church of God, surely it must survive in thee; for to whom should it more belong to die and sacrifice all, than to those who are the sons of God.[340]

Second, Spurgeon believed patriotism in a country with a history of Christianity can be mistaken for Christianity itself. Spurgeon, like most other citizens of his country, was proud to be a British citizen. Though he disagreed with a great deal of their domestic and foreign policies, he felt that God had blessed England because of its Christian heritage. Spurgeon came close to combining his patriotism for all things England with Christianity itself in this excerpt from an 1860 sermon:

We are a proud people; no nation upon the earth can match us for boasting. We have larger words to speak concerning our own dignity than any other race of men. It were well for us if we had humbler words before the throne of God. I believe we are a more highly favored nation than even Israel of old. God hath done more for Britain, or certainly as much, as he did for Abraham's race, and even if we have not rebelled and revolted as often as did Israel in the wilderness, yet our little rebellions, if they were so, would be great because of the greatness of God's goodness.[341]

In England (and, one could argue, the United States), the strong belief that God poured out his providential favor on his country to the tune of being a "more highly favored nation than even Israel of old" showed how prevalent the patriotic fervor had afflicted its citizens. In light of England's Great Panic of 1866, Spurgeon reminded his congregation about the problem of allowing patriotic fervor to win the day: "Though it is clear as noonday in Scripture and in experience that stability is not to be found beneath the moon, yet men are for ever building upon earth's quicksand as if it were

---

[340] Spurgeon, "The Sons of God," *NPSP* 6:339 (1860).
[341] Spurgeon, "A Basket of Summer Fruit," *MTP* 6:343 (1860).

substantial rock, and heaping up its dust as though it would not all be blown away."[342]

Third, Spurgeon believed that, while patriotism and nationalism can turn into false idols due to a confused allegiance, God has called his believers as citizens of heaven to engage as citizens of their respective countries. Spurgeon encouraged—nay, demanded—that Christians recognize their role in helping fellow image bearers steward God's creation. The close neighbors Christians must love are those who are fellow citizens of their respective countries.

Fourth, Spurgeon believed Christians should beware of combining the spiritual realm and the earthly (political) realm to resist and remove the temptation of compromising the spiritual for the earthly. Spurgeon's front-row seat to the Anglican Church's marriage with the British government showed in stark terms the combining these two realms, causing him much distress on behalf of the souls of the people.

Fifth, Spurgeon believed that patriotism for one's country in church must be celebrated with caution, for this excludes other countries and the believers within those countries. Spurgeon provided an example of love of country and prayer for those in political authority, but Spurgeon also longed to see the nations come under the submission of the gospel as one. A false priority in citizenship will keep a Christian from the true priority of the Great Commission in making disciples of all nations (Mt 28:18–20).

Sixth, Spurgeon exhorted Christians not to expect the government to meet every need in existence. Part of being a citizen of heaven is loving the neighbors who live with you as fellow citizens of earth and as part of the family of God worldwide, as far as possible. Though engaged in the political process, Spurgeon did not expect the government to follow through in alleviating every single issue. He expected the government to lead based on the truth of Christian principles, but he also led his church to follow through on those same Christian principles and act for the glory of God and where He provided.

---

[342]Spurgeon, "A Lesson from the Great Panic," *MTP* 12:690 (1866).

Lastly, Spurgeon believed citizens of heaven are more connected to one another than citizens of the earth; and those adopted into the family of God are closer than those born merely into a biological family. The eternal nature of the family of God transcends all earthly relationships outside of Christ. Spurgeon often reminded his listeners and readers of the transient nature of whatever this world offers, even this earthly citizenship. "Soon shall all worlds behold the nobility of the service of Christ, for it will bring with it the most blessed of all rewards. When men look back on what they have done for their fellows, how small is the recompense of a patriotic life! The world soon forgets its benefactors."[343]

In connecting this chapter to the thesis, Spurgeon lamented how England, which identified as a Christian nation, used its imperial philosophy to oppress other countries' citizenry to maintain its world domination. Christian's eyes are always on the eternal, not the temporary. As a Christian, should one's nationality inform them more when interacting and engaging those of another nationality than their Christian citizenship, which seeks all as fellow image bearers of God in need of the gospel and as neighbors needing to see the love of Christ, then those Christians and churches should repent.

Summarizing Chapter Four:
Spurgeon's Ethic on Racism

Chapter Four sought to cull certain principles from Spurgeon's preaching to construct a gospel-centered ethic toward the vulnerable in relation to racism. Spurgeon will help the contemporary American church navigate through the troubled waters of racism in their culture and, specifically, within the church.

First, Spurgeon studied diligently both the canon of Scripture and the culture in which he lived. Spurgeon served as a superb example of knowing the ebb and flow of the narrative of Scripture well. While Spurgeon understood the culture of his time, he also noted, "I am afraid that this is a magazine reading age, a newspaper reading age, a periodical reading age, but not so much a

---

[343] Spurgeon, "Our Motto," *MTP* 25:1484 (1879).

Bible reading age as it ought to be."[344] If Spurgeon were writing in the present age, he would likely write, "I am afraid that this is a Facebook-scrolling age, an Instagram-scrolling age, a tabloid-reading age, a pornographic-viewing age..." for what he preached to his people then is the same principle today. He did not take total umbrage in understanding the times (for he was quite adept at the practice), but insomuch as to help the church understand how to apply the gospel. "Be much with the silly novels of the day, and the foolish trifles of the hour, and you will degenerate into vapid wasters of your time; but be much with the solid teaching of God's word, and you will become solid and substantial men and women; drink them in, and feed upon them, and they shall produce in you a Christ-likeness, at which the world shall stand astonished."[345]

Second, Spurgeon's ministry was committed to the idea that every person populating the planet is made in the image of God. When addressing a gospel-centered ethic toward the vulnerable, this serves as a foundational doctrine moving forward. In the category of racism, a recognition that all of humanity, regardless of race, bears God's image and has value must continually drive our preaching and activism.

> Some men conceive that they are to bear the image of Christ to warrant them as being his followers, although their works tell another tale....Now a Christian is not to bear the image of Christ as a penny bears the superscription of the Queen....There is something more required of us... than having in some dark corner the name of Jesus tattooed into the skin of our profession.[346]

Thus, Spurgeon told Christians not only to see others with the *imago Dei* about them but to also act as such—not merely with Christ stamped on us but having something "bestowed upon us by the Spirit."[347]

---

[344] Spurgeon, "How to Read the Bible," *MTP* 25:1503 (1879).

[345] Spurgeon, "The Talking Book," *MTP* 17:1017 (1871).

[346] Spurgeon, "Portraits of Christ," *MTP* 7:355 (1861).

[347] Spurgeon, "Portraits."

Third, Spurgeon found a champion in the culture who encouraged the principle of all people being image bearers of God. That champion was William Wilberforce, who found an adversary in the likes of Charles Darwin. For abolitionists in the States, such champions included Abraham Lincoln (1809–1865); Frederick Douglass (1818–1895); Harriet Tubman (d. 1913), who was the leader of the Underground Railroad, which helped escaped slaves find freedom in the north; and William Lloyd Garrison (1805–1879), an abolitionist and the editor of an abolitionist periodical, *The Liberator*.

For Spurgeon, Wilberforce was the ideal champion not solely for his activism but for the Christianity that propelled him. For the United States, preachers such as Theodore Weld (1803–1895), whose work *American Slavery As It Is: Testimony of a Thousand Witnesses* (co-authored by his wife Angelina Grimke and her sister Sarah Grimke)[348], and Charles Finney (1792–1876), aided another evangelical abolitionist, Harriet Beecher Stowe (1811–1896) with her seminal work, *Uncle Tom's Cabin*.[349] Yet no parallel existed for the church in America whose Christianity dominated their thinking as a politician in the way Wilberforce did for the churches of England (dissenting or otherwise). Thus, some Americans had to look across the ocean (as did Frederick Douglass) to find their champion in Wilberforce.

Fourth, Spurgeon's hermeneutics were influenced by the redemptive arc of Scripture, not by the surrounding cultural worldviews. In a sermon from which this chapter has already quoted, Spurgeon remarked how our minds must be prepared to read the Scriptures:

> We are not always fit, it seems to me, to read the Bible. At times it were well for us to stop before we open the volume. "Put off thy shoe from thy foot, for the place whereon thou standest is holy ground." You have just come in from careful thought and anxiety about your worldly business, and you cannot

---

[348] Weld, *American Slavery As It Is: Testimony of a Thousand Witnesses*.
[349] Stowe, *Uncle Tom's Cabin or, Life Among the Lowly*.

immediately take that book and enter into its heavenly mysteries.[350]

Spurgeon sought to have his congregation (and all others, for that matter) read the Scriptures on God's own terms rather than reading them through the lens of our "worldly business."

Spurgeon ultimately preached that the Bible was about the redemptive arc of Scripture that culminated in the person of Jesus Christ:

> Most of the historical books were intended to be types either of dispensations, or experiences, or offices of Jesus Christ. Study the Bible with this as a key, and you will not blame [George] Herbert when he calls it "not only the book of God, but the God of books." One of the most interesting points of the Scriptures is their constant tendency to display Christ; and perhaps one of the most beautiful figures under which Jesus Christ is ever exhibited in sacred writ, is the Passover Paschal Lamb.[351]

As noted previously in this chapter, the advocacy of slavery in the American Southern churches was due to hermeneutics that veered off-course from exegesis into eisegesis.

Fifth, God does not elect a particular group to adoption but elects a people in Christ from every tribe, tongue, people, and nation. Spurgeon's preaching on the difficult doctrine of election not only brought glory to God for one's salvation but also developed a brotherhood among believers regardless of strata or station in life— or in any era of time:

> The motley throng within these walls is but as a grain of sand, compared with the sea-shore [*sic*], to the multitudes that will then be congregated. Gather ye! gather ye! ye that have been dead these six thousand years. Gather ye! gather ye! ye that were drowned in Noah's flood. Gather ye! gather ye! all ye hosts of Egypt, and ye myriads of Chaldea, and of Babylon, of Persia,

---

[350] Spurgeon, "How to Read the Bible," *MTP* 25:1503 (1879).

[351] Spurgeon, "Christ Our Passover," *NPSP* 2:54. Spurgeon quoted from the poet George Herbert (1593–1633) in his book *The Critical Heritage*, 210.

and of Greece. Gather ye! ye legions of Rome! ye myriads of the middle ages! ye countless millions of China and of swarthy Hindostan, and you of the world across the sea! Gather ye! gather ye! men of every skin and every tongue![352]

God's electing work, accomplished by Christ and applied by the Holy Spirit, shows no partiality! This brought Spurgeon great joy— a joy that he sought to convey to his congregation at the Metropolitan Tabernacle and ultimately to all generations after who would read his work.

In connecting this chapter to the thesis, racism occurs when one race shows partiality and superiority over another race and, to Spurgeon, was the antithesis to Christianity. Racial identity should not lead to a position of vulnerability, especially in a nation that claimed to hold to Christianity. As discussed earlier, the thread of the doctrine of the *imago Dei* continues to inform the Christian's thinking and actions toward those of a different demographic—in this case, those of a different race or nation. Racism affects attitudes toward refugees, immigrants, and even students coming from foreign lands to study. Coming as a citizen of one country to another can be a harrowing proposition for anyone without additional hardships brought on by others. While many come into, say, the United States, for various motives, followers of Jesus should look at them, first, as image bearers of God.

Summarizing Chapter Five:
Spurgeon's Ethic on Religious Liberty

Chapter Five examined Spurgeon's preaching regarding religious liberty and freedom of conscience. Spurgeon saw that those who did not adhere to or join the Church of England were at a societal disadvantage on many fronts. As one who identified with the Nonconformist camp, such as Spurgeon himself, were on the receiving end of intolerance. He thereby identified with the vulnerable who could not ascend with the same advantages that an

---

[352] Spurgeon, "Shiloh," *MTP* 20:1157 (1874).

Anglican possessed. Spurgeon sought freedom of conscience regarding religious liberty.

First, Spurgeon recognized that Christians have fought for religious liberty throughout Christian history. Religious liberty has stood for two millennia as a conviction of Christian religion. This conviction stands as a principle evolving from an inbred understanding about the rights of all men to live according to their consciences. Spurgeon resolutely believed that this was a belief worth fighting for.

Second, Spurgeon believed that Christians who desire to possess religious liberty must also dispense religious liberty. Spurgeon's preaching and understanding of both British and American history displayed the hypocrisy of those authorities who fought for religious liberty for themselves but then failed to provide that same religious liberty to their citizens (as shown when the Church of England broke away from Rome in 1534 and when Colonial America broke away from England in the 1770s). If one wishes to possess religious liberty, then one must fight for the same provision for others.

Third, Spurgeon believed that Christians must discern what religious liberty truly entails. Spurgeon clearly preached that freedom of religion did not mean freedom from religion. Those mistakes in understanding were made by his own contemporaries as they are made today—mistakes made in both the private and the public spheres.

Fourth, Spurgeon believed that nations that observe and provide religious liberty are more receptive to the gospel. While Spurgeon fought for religious freedom for all, he also saw the immediate benefit of propagating his own religious convictions. Ultimately, Spurgeon was not a universalist who believed that everyone would ultimately go to heaven, but was an evangelical who believed that the only way to have eternal life was to receive Christ as Lord.

Lastly, nations that provide freedom of conscience about religion are more apt to provide liberty for all. Every citizen of a nation has the right to freedom of conscience. If one group of people does not have these freedoms, then other groups do not have assurances of freedom to pursue the dictates of their own conscience.

In connecting this chapter to the thesis, Spurgeon repeatedly noted that he wanted "equal footing for all religions." Those who suffered under the oppression of the Church of England sat in a position of vulnerability. Spurgeon knew that with his position of influence as the leading Nonconformist in England, he needed to stand as an advocate for those who had little to no voice.

Insights for Ministry from Spurgeon's Works

In examining the various principles derived from Spurgeon's views regarding patriotism/nationalism, racism, and religious liberty, this section focuses on:

First, a gospel-centered ethic in ministry must be rooted in a strong theology. Spurgeon never forsook the preaching of the Word and the regenerative work of the gospel when addressing any form of work inside or outside the church. Grounding this ethic in the preaching of the Word and in the gospel prevents developing a sloppy hermeneutic based on the traditions and preferences of any culture rather than of Christ. Having this foundation would help the church avoid the interpretive problems that flummoxed the American South regarding racism and Spurgeon's own denomination in England regarding hermeneutics such as the higher critical method and the welcoming of Darwinism and natural selection.

In each of the issues addressed in this work, the thread of the doctrine of the *imago Dei* played a prominent role. Since God created all humanity in His image, every person who comes across the path of a believer or church is seen as valuable and loved enough to share the gospel of Christ. Thus, a church must be grounded in a strong biblical foundation that promotes a high view of God, a strong view of Scripture, and a compelling view of the life-changing gospel for all.

Second, Christians should welcome and minister to those from other demographics: other races, immigrants, refugees, and foreign students coming to study. Patriotism, as Spurgeon believed, was an admirable quality out of love for the country in which God had providentially placed that citizen. However, this quality is not admirable when morphs from the love of a country to a feeling of superiority over citizens of other countries. Spurgeon understood the ill effects that came upon the immigrants and refugees who spilled over into London in the wake of the Irish Famine of the late 1840s. Spurgeon saw the orphans in the street and the struggles of families to make ends meet. Yet, Spurgeon preached the Scriptures and saw what the Scriptures said about sojourners and strangers going through Israel and how God's people were to minister to them because they themselves were rescued as strangers in a strange land. Spurgeon reminded his people that they too were aliens and strangers:

> As many of us as have believed in Christ have been called out. The very meaning of a church is, "called out by Christ." We have been separated. I trust we know what it is to have gone without the camp, bearing Christ's reproach. Henceforth, in this world we have no home, no true home for our spirits; our home is beyond the flood; we are looking for it amongst the unseen things; we are strangers and sojourners as all our fathers were, dwellers in this wilderness, passing through it to reach the Canaan which is to be the land of our perpetual inheritance.[353]

Christians, representing every type of citizen from every nation, are themselves citizens of a better country (cf. Heb 11:15–16) who are passing through a foreign land as sojourners on their way home to the Promised Land. Therefore, as foreign citizens here on earth, Christians look for ways to minister and help those who are foreign citizens in other countries in their vulnerability and downtrodden condition.

Third, even as citizens of heaven, Christians must infiltrate every sphere of culture to not only bring the gospel but to also give a voice to the voiceless in society. Spurgeon studied not only the text of Scripture but also the context of his culture. Part of this study seeing God's perspective on the vulnerable but also seeing the

---

[353] Spurgeon, "The Pilgrim's Longings," *MTP* 18:1030 (1872).

vulnerable who have no voice and, out of compassion for them and a recognition of their status as fellow image bearers of God, providing a mechanism for them to be heard, cared for, and to provide an advocate for the cause of Christ and the love of neighbor.

Fourth, when the vulnerable are under systemic oppression, Christians should not avoid speaking out in the political realm. Many evangelical churches shy away from speaking on matters of injustice and oppression that have been appropriated by politicians. Spurgeon's political leanings were informed by his ethic toward the vulnerable. This work has given numerous examples of Spurgeon's preaching and writing that address matters that many in modern American times would be considered off-limits due to many churches' non-profit status.[354] Sadly, many use this restriction to avoid any stance on any issue addressed in the political arena (although the IRS does not forbid this, only siding with candidates or any type of "voter education or registration activities with evidence of bias" is forbidden and could result in a loss of the organization's tax-exempt status).[355]

Spurgeon shows modern-day evangelicals that Christians should stand at the forefront of issues that move against the vulnerable or preferring one group over another. For example, Christians taking a stance against abortion laws and promoting adoption options, systemic racism, undercutting religious liberty, and unfair immigration laws are modern examples of the church growing more and more involved in politics and using their voice not only as citizens of their respective countries but as citizens of an eternal Kingdom.

---

[354] "The Restriction of Political Campaign Intervention by Section 501(c)(3) Tax-Exempt Organizations." "Under the Internal Revenue Code, all section 501(c)(3) organizations are absolutely prohibited from directly or indirectly participating in, or intervening in, any political campaign on behalf of (or in opposition to) any candidate for elective public office. Contributions to political campaign funds or public statements of position (verbal or written) made on behalf of the organization in favor of or in opposition to any candidate for public office clearly violate the prohibition against political campaign activity. Violating this prohibition may result in denial or revocation of tax-exempt status and the imposition of certain excise taxes."

[355] Ibid.

Fourth, churches should work to reach across all barriers of racial, medical, and economic strata in society to meet both physical and spiritual needs. Spurgeon scholarship documents the sixty-six organizations started out of the Metropolitan Tabernacle to meet the many spiritual and physical needs of the citizens of his city. Spurgeon did not bury his head in his Bible out of an obligation to provide his congregants a sermon on Sunday at the expense of the needs outside of the Tabernacle. While Spurgeon was involved in politics, one is reminded that he did not expect politics to meet every need. Both personally and pastorally through the church, Spurgeon sought to address the needs directly.

Conclusion

This work stemmed from Spurgeon's application of the second part of the Great Commandment, which is to love one's neighbor as oneself. Unlike the antagonists in the Parable of the Good Samaritan who were selective in whom they would care for, Spurgeon took his lead from the Samaritan. Spurgeon preached a sermon on this parable in 1862. This work closes with a quote that started the sermon, simply titled, "Good News for You":

> The good Samaritan is a masterly picture of true benevolence. The Samaritan had no kinship with the Jew, he was purely of foreign origin, yet he pities his poor neighbour. The Jews cursed the Cuthites, and would have no dealings with them, for they were intruders in their land. There was nothing therefore, in the object of the Samaritan's pity that could excite his national sympathies, but everything to arouse his prejudices, hence the grandeur of his benevolence.

> It is not my intention this morning, to indicate the delightful points of excellence which Christ brings out in order to illustrate what true charity will perform. I want you only to notice this one fact, that the benevolence which the Samaritan exhibited towards this poor wounded and half-dead man, was available benevolence. He did not say to him, "If you will walk to Jericho, then I will bind up your wounds, pouring in the oil and wine;"

or, "If you will journey with me as far as Jerusalem, I will then attend to your wants." Oh, no, he came "where he was," and finding that he could do nothing whatever for his own assistance, the good Samaritan began with him there and then upon the spot, putting no impossible conditions to him, proposing no stipulations which the man could not perform, but doing everything for the man, and doing it for him as he was and where he was.[356]

---

[356] Spurgeon, "Good News for You," *MTP* 8:473 (1862).

Bibliography

"3 Ways Spurgeon Conquered His Secret Sin," https://tinyurl.com/2x5rcbac.

"XVII: Religious Liberty," *Baptist Faith and Message (2000)*. Nashville: LifeWay Press, 2000.

Arnold, Matthew. *Culture and Anarchy,* J. Dover Wilson, ed. Cambridge: Cambridge University Press, 1935.

Article XVI of the "Virginia Declaration of Rights," George Mason's Draft, and Final Version, in Dreisach and *Hall, Sacred Rights of Conscience.*

Ashmall, Donald H. "Spiritual Development and the Free Church Tradition: The Inner Pilgrimage." *Andover Newton Quarterly 20* (1980).

Bacon, Ernest W. *Spurgeon: Heir of the Puritans.* Arlington Heights, IL: Christian Liberty Press, 1967.

Bartoletti, Susan Campbell. *Black Potatoes: The Story of the Great Irish Famine, 1845–1850.* New York: Houghton Mifflin Harcourt Publishing Company, 2001.

Bates, Katherine Lee. "America, the Beautiful." Boston: Oliver Ditson Company, 1910.

Bauer, Patricia. *Chariots of Fire,* Warner Bros., 1981.

Bavinck, Herman. *Reformed Dogmatics, Vol. 1.* Grand Rapids: Baker Academic, 2008.

Bebbington, David. *Evangelicalism in Modern Britain: A History from the 1730s to the 1980s.* London: Unwin Hyman, 1989.

———. "Spurgeon and the Common Man." *Baptist Theology and Review*, Spring 1995.

———. *The Dominance of Evangelicalism: The Age of Spurgeon to Moody.* Downers Grove, IL: InterVarsity Press, 2005.

Behe, Michael. *Darwin's Black Box: A Biochemical Challenge to Evolution—10ᵗʰ Anniversary Edition.* New York: Free Press, 2006.

Bellah, Robert N. "Religion in America." Daedalus, *Journal of the American Academy of Arts and Sciences.* Winter 1967.

Blight, David W. *Frederick Douglass: Prophet of Freedom.* New York: Simon & Schuster, 2020.

Burley, A. Cunningham, *Spurgeon and His Friendships.* Norwich, England: Epworth Press, 1933.

Bush, L. Russ, and Tom J. Nettles. *Baptists and the Bible: The Baptist doctrines of biblical inspiration and religious authority in historical perspective.* Chicago: Moody Press, 1980.

Carlile, J.C. *Charles H. Spurgeon.* Westwood, NJ: Barbour and Company, 1987.

Carswell, Robyn. "Charles Spurgeon: The Prince and the Paupers." *Historia* (2005).

Chadwick, Edwin. 1842 *Report on the Sanitary Conditions of the Labouring Population.* Modern English Society—History and Structure, 1842.

Cobbett, William. "Debate on Mr. Wilberforce's Resolutions respecting the Slave Trade." *The Parliamentary History of England: from the Norman Conquest in 1066 to the year 1803.* London: T. Curson Hansard, 1806–1820.

"Constitution of the Confederate States." March 11, 1861. cdli:wiki https://tinyurl.com/3vk3em99.

Curnow, Tim; Erroll Hulse; David Kingdon; and Geoff Thomas. *A Marvelous Ministry: How the All-Round Ministry of Charles Haddon Spurgeon Speaks to Us Today.* Ligonier, PA: Soli Deo Gloria Publications, 1993.

Dallimore, Arnold, *Spurgeon: A New Biography.* Carlisle, PA: Banner of Truth Trust, 1985.

Darwin, Charles. *On The Origin of Species by Means of Natural Selection, or Preservation of Favoured Races in the Struggle for Life.* London: John Murray, 1859.

———. *The Descent of Man.* New York: D. Appleton and Company, 1889.

Davies, Horton. "Expository Preaching: Charles Haddon Spurgeon," *Foundations* 6 (1963).

————. *Worship and Theology in England, Book 2: From Watts to Wesley to Martineau, 1690–1900.* Grand Rapids: Eerdmans Publishing Company, 1996.

Day, Richard Ellsworth. *The Shadow of the Broad Brim.* Philadelphia: Judson Press, 1934.

Douglass, Frederick. "The Pro-Slavery Mob and the Pro-Slavery Ministry," *Douglass' Monthly,* March 1861.

Douglass, Frederick. "What Shall Be Done if the Slaves are Emancipated?" *Douglass' Monthly,* January 1862.

Drummond, Lewis. *Spurgeon: Prince of Preachers.* Grand Rapids: Kregel Publications, 1992.

Duke, David Nelson. "Charles Haddon Spurgeon: Social Concern Exceeding an Individualistic, Self-Help Ideology." *Baptist History and Heritage, 22:4* (1987).

Estep, William. "The Making of a Prophet: An Introduction to Charles Haddon Spurgeon." *Baptist History and Heritage,* 19:4 (1984).

Eswine, Zack. *Spurgeon's Sorrows: Realistic Hope for Those Who Suffer from Depression.* Ross-shire, Scotland: Christian Focus Publications, 2014.

Fant, Jr., Clyde and William M. Pinson. VI, *20 Centuries of Great Preaching.* Waco, TX: Word, 1971.

Ferguson, Duncan. "The Bible and Protestant Orthodoxy: The Hermeneutics of Charles Spurgeon," *Journal of the Evangelical Theological Society* 25:4. December 1982.

Firth, Charles. *Oliver Cromwell and the Rule of the Puritans in England.* London: Putnam Son's, 1900.

Fullerton, W.Y., *Charles Spurgeon: A Biography.* London: Williams and Norgate, 1920.

George, Christian. "An analysis of the doctrine of the priesthood of Jesus Christ in the functional Christology of Charles Haddon Spurgeon," *Theology in Scotland* (2011).

————. "Jesus Christ, The 'Prince of Pilgrims': A Critical Analysis of the Ontological, Functional, and Exegetical Christologies in the Sermons, Writings, and Lectures of Charles Haddon Spurgeon (1834–1892)." https://tinyurl.com/2ex5csxd.

Glover, Willis B. "English Baptists at the Time of the Downgrade Controversy," *Foundations,* 6 (1963).

Gregory, Joel. "Spurgeon's Resignation from the British Baptist Union: *A Microhistory of First Responders." Baptist History and Heritage* (Fall 2018).

Hall, J.D. "Spurgeon as I Knew Him." *Review & Expositor* 16:1 (1919).

Harmon, Jerry, "The Soteriology of Charles Haddon Spurgeon,"

Hayden, Eric. *Spurgeon on Revival.* Grand Rapids: Zondervan, 1962.

Herberg, Will. *Protestant-Catholic-Jew.* Garden City, N.Y.: Doubleday & Co., 1955.

Hixson, Elijah. "New Testament Textual Criticism in the Ministry of Charles Haddon Spurgeon." *Journal of the Evangelical Theological Society* 57/3 (2014).

Hopkins, Mark. *Nonconformity's Romantic Generation: Evangelical and Liberal Theologies in Victorian England.* Wipf and Stock Publishers, 2007.

Horton, Michael. *Christless Christianity: The Alternative Gospel of the American Church.* Grand Rapids: Baker Books, 2008.

Jefferson, Thomas. "Jefferson's Letter to the Danbury Baptists." *Information Bulletin.* June 1998, 57:6. https://tinyurl.com/3sp8tdyd.

Johnson, Phillip E. *Darwin on Trial.* Downers Grove, IL: InterVarsity Press, 1993.

Kenny, Kevin ed. *Ireland and the British Empire.* Oxford: Oxford University Press, 2006.

Kidd, Thomas S. *What is an Evangelical? The History of a Movement in Crisis.* New Haven, CT: Yale University Press, 2019.

Kidd Thomas S. and Barry Hankins. *Baptists in America.* New York: Oxford University Press, 2015.

Kinealy, Christine. *This Great Calamity: The Irish Famine 1845–52.* Dublin, Ireland: Gill & Macmillan, 1994.

King Jr., Martin Luther. *Strength to Love.* New York: Harper & Row, 1963.

Kruppa, P.S. *Charles Haddon Spurgeon: A Preacher's Progress.* New York: Garland, 1982.

Letters of Charles Haddon Spurgeon. Edinburgh, Scotland: The Banner of Truth Trust, 1992.

"Lewis Drummond." https://tinyurl.com/kj7x6wj4.

Macartney, George. *An Account of Ireland in 1773. By a Late Chief Secretary of that Kingdom.* Farmington Hills, MI: Gale ECCO, 2010.

Magnus, Philip. *Gladstone, A Biography.* New York: E.P. Dutton and Company, 1954.

McMullen, Michael D. "William Wilberforce: 'Agent of Usefulness.'" *Midwestern Journal of Theology* 18.2 (2019).

Meacham, Jon. *American Gospel: God, the Founding Fathers, and the Making of a Nation.* New York: Random House, 2006.

Meredith, Albert R. *The Social and Political Views of C.H. Spurgeon, 1834–1892.* Unpublished Ph.D. study, Michigan State University, 1973.

Merritt, Jonathan. "Defining 'Evangelical.'" *The Atlantic.* cdli:wiki https://tinyurl.com/3ndk2y8p.

Miller, Steve. *C.H. Spurgeon on Leadership.* Chicago: Moody Publishers, 2003.

Mississippi Free Trader, 27 February 1860.

Morden, Peter J. "C.H. Spurgeon and Prayer," *Evangelical Quarterly* 84.4 (2012).

———. "C.H. Spurgeon and Suffering," ERT (2011) 35:4.

———. *C.H. Spurgeon: The People's Preacher.* Surrey, England: CWR, 2009.

———. *Communion with Christ and His People.* Eugene, OR: Pickwick Publications, 2014.

Morris, Henry. *The Twilight of Evolution.* Grand Rapids: Baker Books, 1963.

Murray, Iain H. *Spurgeon V. Hyper-Calvinism: The Battle for Gospel Preaching.* Edinburgh, Scotland: Banner of Truth Trust, 2002.

Najar M., "'Meddling with Emancipation': Baptists, Authority, and the Rift over Slavery in the Upper South," *The Best American History Essays 2007.* New York: Palgrave MacMillan.

Nettles, Tom. *Living By Revealed Truth: The Life and Pastoral Theology of Charles Haddon Spurgeon*. Ross-shire, Scotland: Christian Focus Publications, 2013.

Nicholls, Mike. *Lights to the World: History of Spurgeon's College, 1865–1992*. Self-published, 1994.

Noll, Mark A. *America's God: From Jonathan Edwards to Abraham Lincoln*. Oxford: University Press, 2002.

Oliver, Robert. *History of the English Calvinistic Baptists 1771–1892: From John Gill to C.H. Spurgeon*. Edinburgh, Scotland: Banner of Truth Trust, 2006.

Ort, Phillip. "Sermon of the Week: No. 1099, The Man of Sorrows," cdli:wiki. https://tinyurl.com/v7f95v4x.

Ort, Phillip; Timothy Gatewood; and Edward Romine. "Charles Spurgeon: The Quintessential Evangelical." *Midwestern Journal of Theology* 18:1 (2019).

Pike, Godfrey Holden. *Charles Haddon Spurgeon*. London: Cassell and Company Limited, 1893.

Piper, John. "Charles Spurgeon: Preaching Through Adversity." *21 Servants of Sovereign Joy: Faithful, Flawed, and Fruitful*. Wheaton, IL: Crossway Books, 2018.

Prothero, Stephen. *American Jesus: How the Son of God Became a National Icon*. New York: Farrar, Straus and Giroux, 2003.

———. *Why Liberals Win the Culture Wars (Even When They Lose Elections): The Battles That Define America from Jefferson's Heresies to Gay Marriage*. San Francisco: HarperOne, 2016.

Randall, Ian M. "C.H. Spurgeon (1834–1892): A Lover of France." *EJT* 24:1 (2015).

Ray, Charles. *The Life of Charles Haddon Spurgeon*. London: Passmore and Alabaster, 1903.

Rose, Nathan. "Spurgeon and the Slavery Controversy of 1860: A Critical Analysis of the Anthropology of Charles Haddon Spurgeon, as it relates specifically to his Stance on Slavery." *Midwestern Journal of Theology*: 16:1 (2017).

Scarberry, Mark S. "John Leland and James Madison: Religious Influence on the Ratification of the Constitution and on the Proposal of the Bill of Rights." *Penn State Law Review* 113:3 (2009).

Schaaffhausen, Herrmann. *Anthropologgischer Anzeiger; Bericht uber die biologisch-anthropologische Literatur.* 50:4, 1992.

Schaff, Philip. *Slavery and the Bible: A Tract for the Times.* Chambersberg, PA: M. Kieffer & Co.'s Caloric Printing Press, 1861.

Skinner, Craig. "The Preaching of Charles Haddon Spurgeon." *Baptist History and Heritage,* 19:4.

Smith, Christian and Melinda Lundquist Denton, *Soul Searching: The Religious and Spiritual Lives of American Teenagers.* London: Oxford University Press, 2005.

Smith, Dale Warren. *The Victorian Preacher's Malady: The Metaphorical Usage of Gout in the Life of Charles Haddon Spurgeon.*

Spurgeon, "A Basket of Summer Fruit," *NPSP* 6:343 (1860).

————. "A Great Mistake and the Way to Rectify It," *MTP* 28 (1882).

————. "A Happy Christian," *MTP* 13:176.

————. "A Lesson from the Great Panic," *MTP* 12:690 (1866).

————. "A New Order of Priests and Levites," 17:992.

————. "A Peal of Bells," *MTP* 7:399 (1861).

————. "A Sabbath in Paris," *The Baptist Magazine*, February 1862.

————. "Adoption," *MTP* 7:360.

————. "Adoption, the Spirit, and the Cry," *MTP* 24:1435 (1878).

————. *An All-Around Ministry.* Edinburgh: The Banner of Truth Trust, 1960.

————. "An Earnest Invitation," *MTP* 5:260 (1859).

————. "All for Jesus," *MTP* 20:1205 (1874).

————. *Autobiography,* 4 volumes. London: Passmore & Company, 1892.

————. "Certain Singular Subjects," *MTP 29:1718.*

————. "Charity and Purity," *MTP* 39:2313 (1889).

————. "Children Brought to Christ, Not to the Font," *MTP* 10:581 (1864).

————. "Christ Our Passover," *NPSP* 2:54 (1855).

————. "Christ the Overcomer of the World," *MTP* 22:1327 (1876).

———. "Christ's Universal Kingdom, and how it cometh," *MTP* 26:1585 (1880).

———. "Citizenship in Heaven," *MTP* 8:476 (1862).

———. "Corn in Egypt," *MTP* 5:234 (1859).

———. "David Dancing before the Ark Because of His Election," *MTP* 34:2031 (1888).

———. "Divine Sovereignty," *NPSP* 2:77 (1856).

———. "Effects of Sound Doctrine," *NPSP* 6:324 (1860).

———. "Election," *MTP* 1:41–42 (1855).

———. "Election No Discouragement to Seeking Souls," *MTP* 10:553 (1864).

———. "Fast-Day Service," *NPSP* 3:154–55 (1857).

———. "Faith" *NPSP* 3:107 (1856).

———. "Faith versus Sight," *MTP* 12:677.

———. "Faith Working by Love," *MTP* 26:1553 (1880).

———. "Following the Risen Christ," *MTP* 26:1530 (1880).

———. "For Whom Did Christ Die?" *MTP* 20:1191 (1874).

———. "Glorious Predestination," *MTP* 18:1043 (1872).

———. "Good News for You," *MTP* 8:473 (1862).

———. "Hideous Discovery," *MTP* 32:1911 (1886).

———. "Holiness, the Law of God's House," *MTP* 27:1618 (1881).

———. "How to Read the Bible," *MTP* 25:1503 (1879).

———. "India's Ills and England's Sorrows," NPSP 3:150 (1857).

———. "Jesus: All Blessing and All Blest," *MTP* 37:2187 (1891).

———. "Jesus Known by Personal Revelation," *MTP* 34:2041 (1888).

———. "Joy and Peace in Believing," *MTP* 12:692 (1866).

———. "Jubilee Joy; or, Believers Joyful in Their King," *MTP* 33:1968 (1887).

———. *Lectures to My Students, 4 volumes in one.* Pasadena, TX: Pilgrim Publications, 1990.

———. *Morning by Morning, or Daily Readings for the Family or the Closet.* New York: Sheldon and Company, 1867.

———. "Nearness to God," *MTP* 15:851 (1869).

———. "Nevertheless. Hereafter," *MTP* 23:1364–5.

———. "On Commenting," in *Commenting and Commentaries*. Passmore & Alabaster: London, 1893; repr. Pasadena, TX: Pilgrim, 1990.

———. "Once Dead, Now Alive," *MTP* 40:2388 (1888).

———. "Others to be Gathered," *MTP* 24:1437 (1878).

———. "Our Lowly King," *MTP* 31 (1885).

———. "Our Motto," *MTP* 25:1484 (1879).

———. "Our Sympathizing High Priest," 32:1927 (1886).

———. "Pentecost," *MTP* 30:1783 (1884).

———. "Plenteous Redemption," *MTP* 7:351.

———. *Poland*. London: Passmore & Alabaster, 1864.

———. "Portraits of Christ," 7:355 (1861).

———. "Preaching for the Poor," *NPSP* 3:114 (1857).

———. "Self Low, but Christ High," 36:2161 (1890).

———. "Shiloh," *MTP* 20:1157 (1874).

———. "Signs of the Times, *MTP* 19:1135 (1873).

———. "Spiritual Liberty," *MTP* 1:9 (1855).

———. "Storming the Battlements," *MTP* 1:38 (1855).

———. "Temple Glories," *MTP* 7:375–78 (1861).

———. "The Beginning of Months," *MTP* 28:1687 (1882).

———. "The Best War-Cry," *MTP* 29:1709 (1883).

———. "The Bible," *MTP* 1:15 (1855).

———. "The Blood of the Everlasting Covenant," *NPSP* 5:277 (1859).

———. "The Christian's Great Business," *MTP* 19:1130 (1873).

———. "The Cry of the Heathen," *NPSP* 4:189 (1858).

———. "The Ear Bored with the Awl," *MTP* 20:1174 (1874).

———. "The Exaltation of Christ," *NPSP* 2:101 (1856).

———. "The Exodus," *NPSP* 2:55 (1855).

———. "The Father's Dying Love to His Son," *MTP* 35:2117 (1889).

———. "The Final Separation," *MTP* 21:1234.

———. "The Good Samaritan," *MTP* 23:1360 (1877).

———. "The Great Liberator," *MTP* 10:565 (1864).

———. "The Great Supreme," *MTP* 7:367 (1856).

———. "The Greatest Trial on Record," *MTP* 9:495 (1863).

———. "The Holy Spirit and the One Church," *NPSP* 4:167 (1857).

———. "The Independence of Christianity," *NPSP* 3:149 (1857).

————. "The Leading of the Spirit, the Secret Token of the Sons of God," *MTP*: 21:1220.

————. "The Lord—the Liberator." *MTP* 8:484 (1862).

————. "The Majestic Voice," *NPSP* 2:87 (1856).

————. "The Marvellous Magnet," *MTP* 29:1717.

————. "The Missionaries' Charge and Charta," *MTP* 7: 383 (1861).

————. "The New Year's Guest," *MTP* 30:1757 (1883).

————. "The Pilgrim's Longings," *MTP* 18:1030.

————. "The Sad Wonder," *MTP* 16:935 (1870).

————. "The Scales of Judgment," *NPSP* 5:257 (1859).

————. "The Sin-Offering for the Common People," *MTP* 18:1048 (1872).

————. "The Singular Origin of a Christian Man," *MTP* 31:1829 (1885).

————. "The Sons of God," *NPSP* 6:339 (1860).

————. "The Tenderness of Jesus," *MTP* 36:315 (1890).

————. "The True Priesthood, Temple and Sacrifice," *MTP* 23:1376 (1877).

————. "The Story of a Runaway Slave," *MTP* 21:1268.

————. *The Sword and the Trowel.* 1865.

————. "The Talking Book," *MTP* 17:1017 (1871).

————. "The Unbroken Line of True Nobles," *MTP* 21:1260 (1875).

————. "The War of Truth," *MTP* 3:112 (1857).

————. "The Whole Band Against Christ," *MTP* 39:2333 (1889).

————. *Treasury of David*, 3 vols.

————. "Unconditional Surrender," *MTP* 22:1276.

————. "What are the Clouds? *MTP* 1:36 (1855).

————. "What God Cannot Do!", *MTP* 28:92 (1888).

————. "Why Men Reject Christ," *MTP* 42:2463 (1886).

"Spurgeon on Slavery," *Chicago Tribune,* Feb. 3, 1860.

Stead, W.T. "Eminent Radicals out of Parliament." The Weekly Dispatch, No. 5, November 9, 1879.

Stetzer, Ed. "Patriotism and the Church: Answering the Call to Worship God First." *Influence Magazine.* cdli:wiki https://tinyurl.com/55suprf8.

Stowe, Harriet Beecher. *Uncle Tom's Cabin or, Life Among the Lowly*. Boston: John P. Jewett & Company, 1852.

Strachan, Owen. *The Colson Way: Loving Your Neighbor and Living with Faith in a Hostile World*. Nashville: Thomas Nelson Publishers, 2015.

The Book of Common Prayer, and Administration of the Sacraments, and other Rites and Ceremonies of the Church, According to the Use of the Church of England, Together with the Psalter or Psalms of David, Pointed as they are to be sung or said in Churches. Cambridge: The Church of England, 1662.

The Ideas of Biology. New York: Harper & Brothers, 1962.

"The Restriction of Political Campaign Intervention by Section 501(c)(3) Tax-Exempt Organizations." https://tinyurl.com/nhj9r7ka.

The Southern Reporter and Daily Commercial Courier. April 10, 1860.

Tocqueville, Alexis de. *Democracy in America*. Ed. and trans. Harvey Claflin Mansfield and Delba Winthrop. Chicago: University of Chicago Press, 2000.

Underwood, A.C. *A History of the English Baptists*. London: The Baptist Union of Great Britain and Ireland, 1947.

Vincent, Henry. "Nonconformity," *MTP* 7:399 (1861).

————. The Story of the Commonweal: The Complete and Graphic Narrative of the Origin and Growth of the Movement. Chicago: W.B. Conkey, 1894.

Wax, Trevin. "Why Younger Evangelicals May Feel Uneasy in a Patriotic Church Service." https://tinyurl.com/yvf99jtf, July 2, 2014.

Wayland, Heman Lincoln. *Charles H. Spurgeon: His Faith and Works*. Philadelphia: American Baptist Publication Society, 1892.

Weld, Theodore Dwight. *American Slavery As It Is: Testimony of a Thousand Witnesses*. New York: The American Anti-Slavery Society Office, 1839.

White, "Biblical Ethics," *Evangelical Dictionary of Theology, Second Edition*, ed. Walter Elwell. Grand Rapids: Baker Academic, 2001

————. "Christian Ethical Systems." *Evangelical Dictionary of Theology,* Second Edition, ed. Walter Elwell. Grand Rapids: Baker Academic, 2001.

Wilberforce, R.I., and S. *The Life of William Wilberforce,* Vol 5. London, 1838.

Wilberforce, William. *An Appeal to the Religion, Justice, and Humanity of the Inhabitants of the British Empire, in Behalf of the Negro Slaves in the West Indies.* London: J. Hatchard and Son, 1823.

Wilberforce, William. *A Practical View of Christianity.* Peabody, MA: Hendrickson Publishers, 1996.

Wilken, Robert Louis. *Liberty in the Things of God.* New Haven: Yale University Press, 2019.

Wills, Gregory A. *Democratic Religion: Freedom, Authority, and Church Discipline in the Baptist South 1785–1900.* Oxford: Oxford University Press, 1997.

Wills, Gregory. "The Ecclesiology of Charles H. Spurgeon: Unity, Orthodoxy, and Denominational Identity." *Baptist History and Heritage* (Autumn 1999).

Index

AN ESTIMATED 1-IN-3 PEOPLE HAVE EXPERIENCED
RELIGIOUS TRAUMA AT SOME POINT IN THEIR LIFE.
AS MANY AS 20% CURRENTLY SUFFER FROM IT TODAY.

STOP SPIRITUAL ABUSE

Think twice about how
you approach ministry.

LEARN MORE AND GET RESOURCES AT:
WWW.GCRR.ORG/RT

www.ingramcontent.com/pod-product-compliance
Lightning Source LLC
Chambersburg PA
CBHW071356120626
46546CB00002B/721